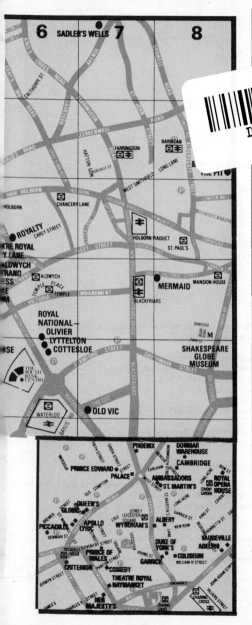

Street
M

**London
Theatreland**
     page 1

**Central
London**
    pages 11-19

**Where
to Eat**
    pages 149-163

KEY

 BRITISH RAIL
NETWORK SOUTHEAST
STATION

 NIGHT BUS

🅿 CAR PARK

◼ THEATRE

 LEICESTER SQUARE
1/2 PRICE
TICKET BOOTH

⊖ UNDERGROUND
STATION

1

Whilst every care has been taken to ensure accuracy the publisher cannot be held responsible for errors resulting from inaccurate information received.

Published and produced by Frank Cook Travel Guides,
8 Wykeham Court, Old Perry Street, Chislehurst, Kent BR7 6PN
Edited by Susan Elms, Eileen Wilsher and Frank Cook
Illustrated by Clive Desmond and Pat Hawley
Printed in Britain by CW Printing, Kent
Phototypeset by Keyset Video Ltd., Woolwich SE18

London maps by Peter Hale, based on the Ordnance Survey Map with the sanction of the Controller of Her Majesty's Stationery Office, copyright reserved.

Copyright © 1979 Frank Cook Travel Guides. All rights reserved. 4th Edition 1990.

In compiling this Guide we would like to make particular mention to the following publications which have proved invaluable to our research:
"The Theatres of London" by Raymond Mander and Joe Mitchelson,
"Victorian & Edwardian Theatres" by Victor Glasstone,
"The Penguin Dictionary of Theatre" by John Russell Taylor,
Lytton's Theatre Seating Plans published by the Dancing Times Lda.

We would also like to thank The Society of West End Theatre for their interest and valuable assistance.

ISBN 09506503-3-1

THE LONDON THEATRE SCENE

"

HOW MANY TIMES have you planned to visit the theatre, made reservations by phone and wondered whether you had booked the best available seat. So often reservations can be a stab in the dark where the awful truth only dawns on arrival in the auditorium. **A book which takes the guesswork out of theatregoing has just been published** entitled *The London Theatre Scene* by Susie Elms, it is published by **Frank Cook Travel Guides.** This neat little paperback not only provides auditorium seating plans of all major London theatres, but also provides street maps, details of how to book and how to get there by public transport. Additionally the guide lists places to eat and stay in and around London's theatreland.

"

Theatre Print-Programmes 1979

NOW INTO ITS 4TH EDITION

FRANK COOK PUBLICATIONS

Contents

Theatres – Concert Halls – Other Venues

Box Office Telephone Numbers:
(Please add prefix 071 when dialling from outside the London Area)

Outer London theatres

Ashcroft, Park Lane, Croydon, Surrey.   Tel: 081-688 9291
Churchill, High Street, Bromley, Kent.   Tel: 081-460 6677
Greenwich, Crooms Hill, SE10.   Tel: 081-858 7755
Hampstead, Swiss Cottage Centre, NW3.   Tel: 071-722 9301
Richmond, The Green, Richmond, Surrey.   Tel: 081-940 0088
Shaw, 100 Euston Road, NW1.   Tel: 071-388 1394
Wimbledon, The Broadway, Wimbledon, SW19.   Tel: 081-540 0362

General Booking Information

Times have changed for booking tickets!

Box office facilities have undoubtedly improved, however an alternative is to telephone one of the reputable ticket agencies which have the advantage of being open when box offices close; some even offer 24 hour service 7 days a week!

Agencies can give details of **seat location which may be easily checked against the identical 'London Theatre Scene' seating plans.** They are able to suggest other shows should your first choice not be available with computerised efficiency. Tickets may be posted or left for collection at the box office. Booking fees are sometimes necessary in providing this enhanced service, and amongst most reputable agencies is about 20% of the ticket price. Sometimes there is no booking fee! Agency telephone numbers are usually listed in newspapers and in the free fortnightly 'Society of West End Theatre Guide'. (For further theatre-booking information concerning the activities of the *Society of West End Theatre* see pages 7-10).

Two leading and reputable ticket agencies are:

KEITH PROWSE established since 1780 have a national network of over 80 retail shops (30 ticket shops in London and 50 travel shops throughout the UK) In addition there is a credit card reservation service – **081-741 999 from 9am until 10pm,** and shops are generally open from 9am until 6pm. **(Tel. 071-629 0346 for your nearest ticket shop).** They are also established in New York, Toronto, Sydney, Auckland, Amsterdam, Jersey and Dublin, operating a worldwide tour and travel service (packages which include tickets for all the hit shows!) They have tickets available for theatres, concerts, sport and major events with instantly confirmed bookings.

TICKETMASTER is a long established computerised ticket retailing company that sells tickets for theatre, rock and pop concerts, exhibitions and other entertainment **on a 24 hour basis 7 days a week. Tel: 071-379 4444.** They also operate a network of retail outlets throughout the country mainly in travel agents including W.H. Smith Exchange Travel, American Express Travel, Co-op Travelcare, Woodcock Travel and John Hilary Travel which have a computerised system offering a wide range of entertainment and instant booking confirmation.

THE SOCIETY OF WEST END THEATRE AT <u>YOUR</u> SERVICE

The Society of West End Theatre, Bedford Chambers,
The Piazza, Covent Garden, London WC2E 8HQ.
Tel: 071-836 3193. Fax: 071-497 2543

Founded by Sir Charles Wyndham in 1908, the Society of West End Theatre (SWET) is the Employers' Association representing the owners, producers and managers of London's 50 West End theatres including the major state-supported national companies. The Marketing Office of SWET works to promote West End theatre to audiences at home and abroad through the following:

The London Theatre Guide
Published every two weeks, the London Theatre Guide is the definitive and comprehensive listing of all West End shows providing complete booking information for groups and individuals, start and finish times, seat facilities for the disabled, and a map of Theatreland. The Guide is available free at all West End theatres, tourist and travel centres, many hotels and libraries – or by individual subscription or in bulk from SWET.

Theatreline
This recorded telephone service provides complete information on all aspects of theatregoing plus daily seat availability by individual theatres or by category of production (musicals, plays, comedies, thrillers, children's theatre or opera/ballet/dance). For Theatreline telephone numbers, see listing in this book, the London Theatre Guide, or pick up a free Theatrecard from theatre box offices. (Calls cost 25p (off peak) or 38p at all other times per minute inc VAT from anywhere in the UK.)

How to Book Theatre Tickets

★ **Go in person to the Theatre Box Office** – generally open from 10.00 am until the start of the evening performance. Pay in cash, by credit card, cheque or West End Theatre Gift Tokens.

★ **Write to the Theatre Box Office** – stating the performance you wish to see with alternative dates if possible, and enclosing a cheque, postal order or West End Theatre Gift Tokens, plus self-addressed stamped envelope.

★ **Telephone the Box Office** – to make a reservation. Then either pay in person or send payment, usually within 3 days.

★ **Use your credit card** – most theatres accept credit card bookings by telephone. You will be asked to present your credit card when you collect your tickets. You can also book by credit card at ticket agencies who may add an additional booking fee to the cost of your tickets. Make sure you enquire regarding the additional fee.

★ **Beware of ticket touts** – a ticket should always have its original face value displayed. If you are sold a ticket at more than its face value, and if that value is not made known to you, please let the Society of West End Theatre know by calling 071-836 3193.

The Half Price Ticket Booth in Leicester Square

The Half-Price Ticket Booth sells tickets for a wide selection of West End shows, on the day of performance only, at half price. Centrally located in Leicester Square, the Booth is open from Monday to Saturday from 12 noon for matinees and from 2.30 - 6.30 for evening performances. Tickets are limited to 4 per person, for cash only. A service charge of £1.00 is added for tickets with a face value of £5.00 or less; £1.25 for all other tickets.

Senior Citizens Matinee Scheme

Many theatres offer reduced price tickets for matinees to Senior Citizens. These can be booked in advance either by telephone or in person, or just prior to the performance. When you collect your tickets you will be asked to show proof that you are a senior citizen: a bus pass, passport, pensioner's card, etc. is acceptable. Theatres which operate the scheme are identified in the London Theatre Guide by the symbol M.

Senior Citizens wishing to attend evening performances at concessionary prices can also use their identification to purchase tickets just before performance begins at those theatres carrying the symbol S in the London Theatre Guide.

Student and Sixth Form Standby Scheme

Unsold tickets at many theatres are available at a discount to students on presentation of a current student card or a sixth former's card just before the performance. Theatres operating this scheme are identified in the London Theatre Guide with the letter S. To join the Sixth Formers' Standby Scheme, send £1 plus a passport-size photograph to the Society of West End Theatre, Bedford Chambers, The Piazza, Covent Garden, London WC2E 8HQ.

West End Theatre Gift Tokens

Available in vouchers of £1, £5, £10 or £20, with no expiry date, Tokens can be exchanged at 50 West End theatres, the Half-Price Ticket Booth in Leicester Square, the Royal Shakespeare Theatre in Stratford-upon-Avon, Chichester Festival Theatre, Greenwich Theatre, the Theatre Museum in Covent Garden plus important London fringe theatres. Presented in attractive wallets complete with the latest London Theatre Guide, tokens make ideal "welcome to London" or thank you gifts. Trade terms are available for large purchases. For information on purchasing West End Theatre Gift Tokens, call Tokenline 071-379 3395.

Services to the Travel Trade

SWET regularly publishes literature specifically targeted to the travel trade. West End Theatre News is a monthly newsletter featuring editorial copy on new developments in the theatre and a first night list for the forthcoming two months. The Group Booking Information Sheet is a monthly bulletin providing complete information on group booking opportunities at West End shows including show descriptions, group rates, theatre facilities and special theatre-related activities. For a free subscription to either of these publications, contact the SWET Marketing Office. For information on coach parking, contact Metropolitan Coach Advisory Service, 071-230 5332.

The Laurence Olivier Awards

Established in 1976 originally as the Society of West End Theatre Awards, the Olivier Awards are now regarded as the highlight of the theatrical year. They are presented annually by the Society in recognition of distinguished artistic achievement in the West End theatre by panels composed of both members of the public and theatre professionals. The Awards are presented at a public ceremony and televised live on the BBC. For more information about becoming a panelist or attending the Awards, please contact the Marketing Office, 071-836 3193.

Theatreline

The Society of West End Theatre presents Theatreline, a recorded telephone information service, providing callers with full details of all shows performed in the West End plus daily seat availability.

For information on daily seat availability by category of production, call the following numbers:

Plays	0836 430959	Comedies	0836 430961	Children's Shows	0836 430963
Musicals	0836 430960	Thrillers	0836 430962	Opera/Ballet/Dance	0836 430964

For complete information by individual theatre which includes a synopsis, names of leading performers, performance times, prices, complete booking information, travel details and daily seat availability, please call the following numbers:

Please note these are NOT Box Office telephone numbers.

Adelphi	0836 430900	Fortune	0836 430917	Playhouse	0836 430935
Albery	0836 430901	Garrick	0836 430918	Prince Edward	0836 430936
Aldwych	0836 430902	Globe	0836 430919	Prince of Wales	0836 430937
Ambassadors	0836 430903	Haymarket	0836 430920	Queens	0836 430938
Apollo	0836 430904	Her Majesty's	0836 430921	Royal Court	0836 430939
Apollo Victoria	0836 430905	London Palladium	0836 430922	Royal Opera Hse	0836 430911
Barbican		Lyric	0836 430923	Royalty	0836 430940
Theatre	0836 430906	Mermaid	0836 490925	Sadler's Wells	0836 430941
The Pit	0836 430907	National Theatre		Savoy	0836 430942
Cambridge	0836 430908	Olivier	0836 430926	Shaftesbury	0836 430943
Coliseum	0836 430909	Lyttelton	0836 430927	St. Martin's	0836 430944
Comedy	0836 430910	Cottesloe	0836 430928	Strand	0836 430945
Criterion	0836 430912	New London	0836 430929	Vaudeville	0836 430946
Dominion	0836 430951	Old Vic	0836 430930	Victoria Palace	0836 430947
Donmar Warehouse	0836 430913	Open Air	0836 430931	Westminster	0836 430948
Drury Lane	0836 430914	Palace	0836 430932	Whitehall	0836 430949
Duchess	0836 430915	Phoenix	0836 430933	Wyndham's	0836 430950
Duke of York's	0836 430916	Piccadilly	0836 430934		

Calls cost 25p (off peak) or 38p at all other times per minute incl. VAT from anywhere in the UK. Theatreline is presented by the Society of West End Theatre in association with FT Cityline.

How does it all work?

Why not find out by enjoying a backstage tour at the *National Theatre* for instance! They occur daily, 10.15, 12.30, 12.45, 5.30 and 6.00 – except on Olivier matinee days when tour times are different. You can send a stamped addressed envelope for more details to Theatre Tours, Royal National Theatre, South Bank, SE1 9PX, or telephone between 10am and 11pm: 071-633 0880.

If interested in Tours/Clubs, other places to contact are:
Act 1 Theatre Travel Club, Theatreland Tours – 071-494 2304
London Theatre Walks, Tour Guides Ltd – 071-839 7438
Stage by Stage Tours – 071-328 7558
Theatre and Concert Rail Club – 0747 41115
Tour Guides Ltd – 071-839 7438

Maps

Every entry in this guide is pinpointed on detailed street maps pages:
1, 10-17 and pages 149-161.

Symbols:

★ Theatres - Concert Halls

● Hotels, Restaurants, Shops, Sightseeing

⊖ Underground Stations

⊟ British Rail Stations

ⓘ Tourist Information Centres

▪ Parking

Central London

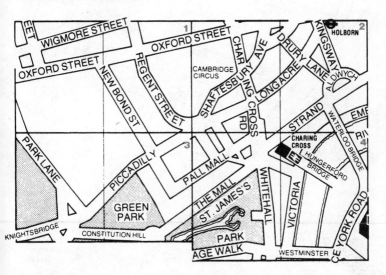

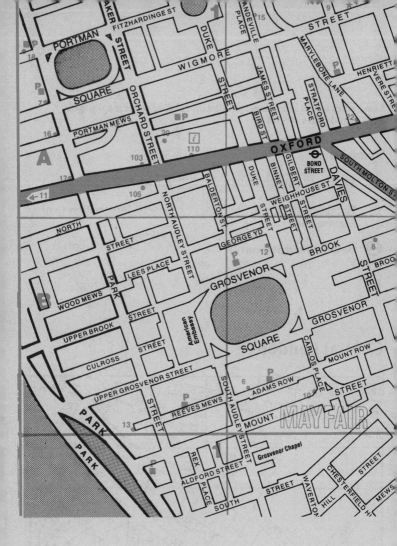

HOTELS:

5	A4	Ramada						
6	B2	Britannia	12	B2	Europa	18	A1	Portman
7	A1	Churchill	13	B1	Grosvenor	19	B4	Regent Palace
8	B2	Claridges	14	A2	Londoner	20	A1	Selfridge
9	A2	Clifton Ford	15	A2	Mandeville	21	A3	St. George's
10	B2	Connaught	16	A1	Mostyn	22	A2	Berkshire
11	A1	Cumberland	17	A1	Mount Royal	23	B3	Westbury

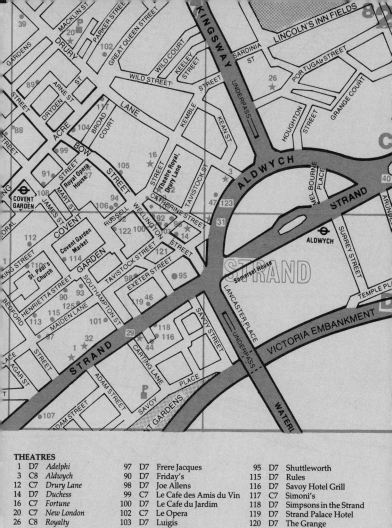

15

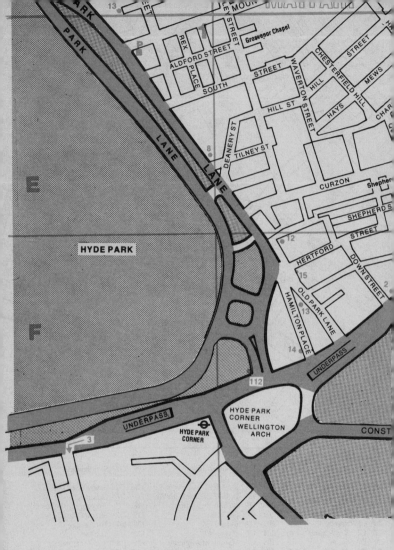

THEATRES:
1 E3 *Mayfair*

HOTELS:

2	F2	Athenaeum
3	F2	Berkeley
4	E3	Holiday Inn Mayfair
5	E3	Brown's
6	E4	Cavendish
7	E2	Chesterfield
8	E1	Dorchester
9	F4	Dukes
11	E3	Green Park
12	F2	Hilton
13	F2	Inn On The Park
14	F2	Intercontinental

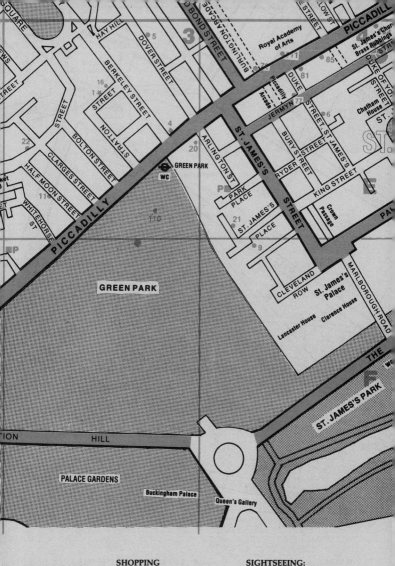

15	F2	Londonderry
16	E3	Mayfair
17	F2	Park Lane
20	E3	Ritz
21	E4	Stafford
22	E3	Washington

SHOPPING

72	E4	Burlington Arcade
77	E4	Dunhill
81	E4	Fortnum & Mason
85	E4	Hatchards
102	E4	Simpson's

SIGHTSEEING:

110	E3	Green Park
111	E4	Royal Academy of Arts
112	F2	Wellington Museum

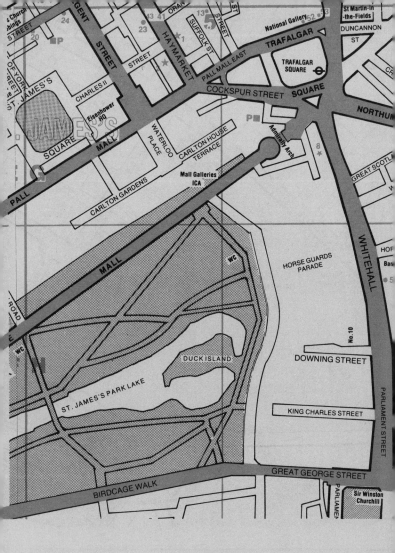

THEATRES:

1	G5	*Haymarket, Theatre Royal*
2	G5	*Her Majesty's*
3	G8	*National*
		Olivier
		Lyttelton
		Cottesloe
4	G8	*South Bank*
		Concert Halls
7	G8	*National Film*
8	G6	*Whitehall*
9	G6	*Player's*
10	G6	*Playhouse*

HOTELS:

11	G6	Charing Cross
12	G6	Royal Adelphi
13	G7	Royal Horseguards
14	G5	Royal Trafalgar

RESTAURANTS:

23	G5, G7	McDonald's
24	G5	Rowleys
33	G6	Sherlock Holmes

SHOPPING:

41	G5	Burberry's
43	G5	Design Centre

SIGHTSEEING:

51	G8	Hayward Gallery
52	G6	National Gallery
53	G6	National Portrait Gallery

Adelphi Theatre

Strand, WC2E 7NH 344-0055

Box Office: 10.00 to 20.00 hrs
Tel: 836 7611/7358
Credit Cards: Yes
Underground: Charing Cross. Buses: 1, 6, 9, 11, 13, 15, 77, 170, 172, 176.

Bars: 5
Seating: 1,500

When seeking a little entertainment in Edwardian times it was fashionable to stroll down the Strand and spend the evening at one of the many theatres, clubs or music halls which abounded. For at the turn of the century, this area around Drury Lane was the heart of lively London. Many of the popular theatres – such as the famous *Gaiety* – have, of course, long since disappeared. But not so *The Adelphi*.

There has been a theatre on the site of the present *Adelphi* since 1806. In 1930 it underwent drastic alterations and today remains much as architect Ernest Schaufelberg designed it.

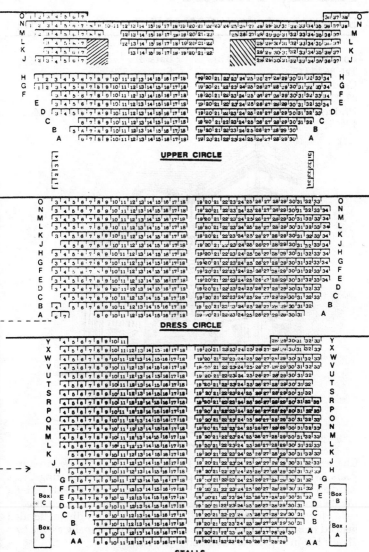

UPPER CIRCLE

DRESS CIRCLE

STALLS

Albery Theatre

St. Martin's Lane, WC2N 4AH

Box Office: 10.00 to 20.00 hrs   Bars: 3
Tel: 867 1115   Seating: 879
Credit Cards: 867 1111
09.00-20.00 hrs
Underground: Leicester Square, Piccadilly Circus. Buses: 1, 24, 29, 176.

Charles Wyndham, manager of *The Criterion Theatre* for twenty-three years, was also the owner of a plot of land between Charing Cross Road and St. Martin's Lane. On the Charing Cross Road side he built the theatre which took his name – and the remainder he planned to sell. However, negotiations fell through and Wyndham decided instead to build another theatre. It was known originally as *The New Theatre* but in 1973 it was changed to *The Albery*.

Albery

The souvenir from the opening night records ". . . on entering the auditorium one is immediately struck with the exquisite lines on which the theatre has been designed, a clear and uninterrupted view of the stage being obtained from literally every part of the theatre . . . the theatre is equipped with all modern and scientific appliances . . ." This is an innovative tradition which continues, for *The Albery* recently became the first theatre in London to introduce electrical flying scenery.

AUDITORIUM PLAN

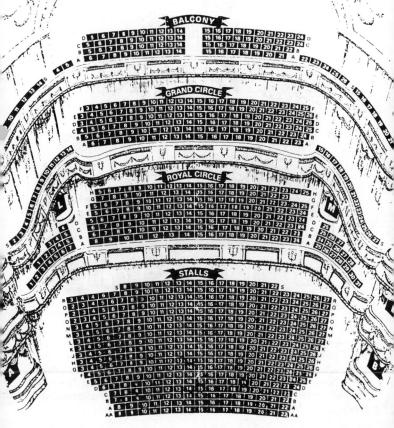

Aldwych Theatre

Aldwych, WC2B 4DF

Box Office: 10.00 to 20.00 hrs   Bars: 3
Tel: 836 6404   Seating: 1,079
Credit Cards: Yes
Underground: Covent Garden, Holborn. Buses: 1, 4, 6, 9, 11, 13, 15, 23, 68, 77, 77A, 170, 171, 172, 176, 188, 501, 502, 513.

At the end of the 19th century when the slums between Drury Lane and Lincoln's Inn were being cleared to make way for two new roads – to be known as The Aldwych and Kingsway – several new theatres were planned. These included two which were to be a "pair" – *The Waldorf* (now *The Strand*) and *The Aldwych*. The decorations are in Georgian style, handsome and ornate.

Aldwych

AUDITORIUM PLAN

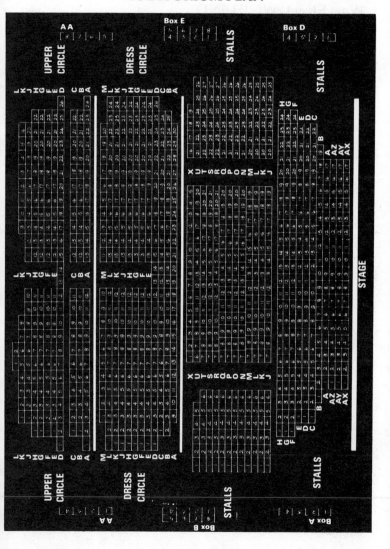

Ambassadors Theatre

West Street, WC2H 9ND

Box Office: 10.00 to 20.00 hrs
Tel: 836 6111/836 3212
Credit Cards: Yes
Underground: Leicester Square.

Bars: 3
Catering: Yes
Seating: 460
Buses: 1, 14, 19, 22, 24, 29, 38, 176.

On 25th November, 1952 a legend began at *The Ambassadors Theatre*. A thriller – destined to run longer than any other play or musical ever performed in Britain – opened. The play, of course, was Agatha Christie's "The Mousetrap" which, after an incredible run, was transferred to *The St. Martin's Theatre* next door in March 1974.

The Ambassadors was built just before the outbreak of the First World War. It is a welcoming little London theatre with a special air of intimacy all its own. *"The Era"* of 7th June, 1913 recorded that ". . . The general scheme of decoration is Louis XVI . . ." and the original style is much the same today, with ambassadorial crests adorning the auditorium.

AUDITORIUM PLAN

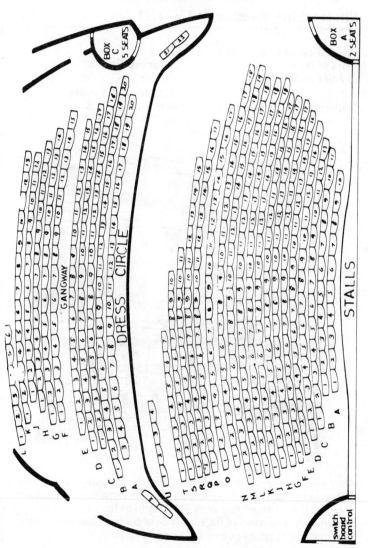

Apollo Theatre

Shaftesbury Avenue, W1V 7HD

Box Office: 10.00 to 20.00 hrs
Tel: 437 2663
Credit Cards: Yes

Bars: 2
Catering: Snacks
Seating: 780
Hearing Aid System

Underground: Piccadilly Circus. Buses: 14, 19, 22, 38.

1887 saw the opening of a new road, which cut through the middle of Soho and which was soon to become synonymous with entertainment – taking precedence over The Strand as the centre of London's theatreland. The name of the road was, of course, Shaftesbury Avenue and one of its first theatres was *The Apollo*. Built in 1905.

Apollo

The Apollo has changed very little over the years. The exterior is in the French Renaissance style and the interior is wonderfully ornate and elegant.

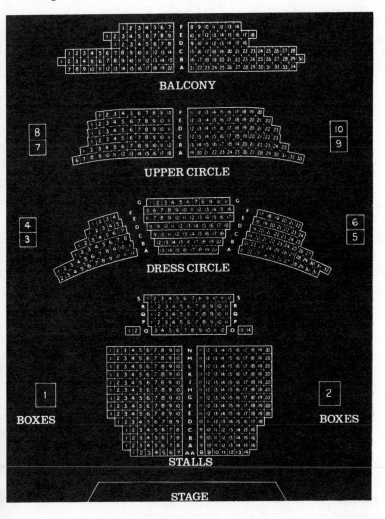

Apollo Victoria Theatre

Wilton Road, SW1

Box Office: 10.00 to 22.00 hrs
Tel: 630 6262
Party Bookings: 828 6188
Credit Cards: Yes

Bars: Open at 18.45
Seating: 2,572
Underground: Victoria.

Built in 1930 as one of the super cinemas of the period, the *New Victoria*, as it was then called, was "a vigorously modern exterior in line with the finest design of the time."

The interior was the work of Trent and Walmsley Lewis and, in its original colours of blue and green, was a highly successful example of the 'atmospheric' auditorium, giving a striking impression of entering an underwater world.

Now redecorated as the *Apollo Victoria* in pink, gold and white, the theatre still retains all its decorative features and plasterwork, and the atmosphere is warm and intimate, belying its size.

Apollo Victoria

The theatre, which is a 'listed building', benefits enormously from its original design for both cinema and stage presentations, combining clear, uncluttered sight lines with all the elaborate technical facilities of the West End.

Audiences have always been struck by the spaciousness of the foyer which runs through the building, giving two identical main entrances at Wilton Road and Vauxhall Bridge Road.

AUDITORIUM PLAN

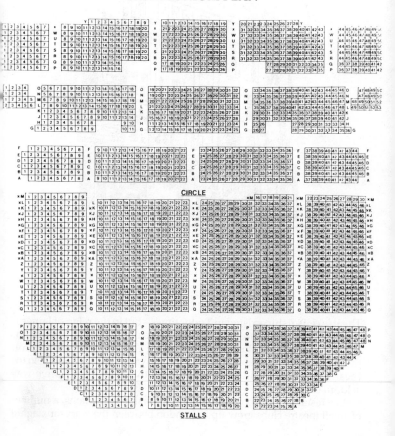

Arts Theatre Club

6/7 Great Newport Street, WC2H 7JA

Box Office: 10.00 to 20.00 hrs
Tel: 836 2132
Credit Cards: Yes
Underground: Leicester Square.

Bars: 1
Catering: Restaurant
Seating: 340
Buses: 1, 24, 29, 176.

Theatre censorship existed in Tudor times – but in the reign of James I, responsibility was placed on the shoulders of the Lord Chamberlain. In 1937, he became the official Licensing Authority for all London theatres (except the Patent theatres), all Royal residences, and also for theatrical societies and clubs – although this latter prerogative was seldom exercised.

As a result of this "loophole" in the censorship regulations, a number of small theatre clubs grew up in London between the wars for staging

Arts Theatre Club

experimental productions. *The Arts Theatre Club*, between St. Martin's Lane and Charing Cross Road opened in 1927. Between 1942 and 1953 the Arts Theatre under Alec Clunes developed a 'pocket National Theatre'. In the mid-fifties Peter Hall presented the premiere of 'Waiting for Godot'. In the mid-sixties the R.S.C. took over. Since 1967 the *Unicorn Theatre* for Children took over and continues as the prime theatre for children in the country, presenting a season of plays each year from September to May for children aged between 4 and 12.

AUDITORIUM PLAN

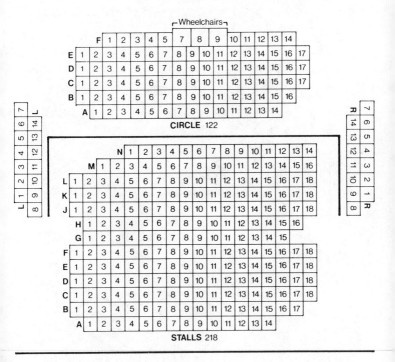

Advance Booking for all
performances
Box Office: 9.00 to 20.00 hrs
Box Office Tel: 638 8891
Recorded Information Service:
628 9760-628 2295

Bars: 7
Catering: Snacks, Selfservice
and Restaurant.

Underground: Moorgate, Barbican, St. Pauls, Bank. Buses: 4, 8,, 9,
11, 21, 25, 43, 76, 133, 141, 214, 271, 502, 503. For Pedestrians: the
main access is at Silk Street, but overground walkway called The
Podium gives access.

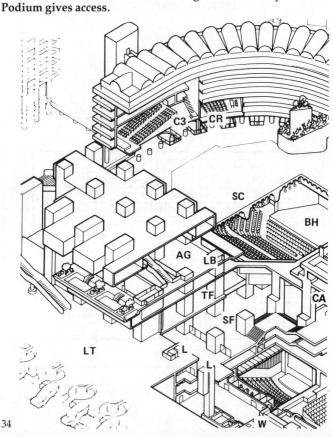

Barbican Centre

"One of the wonders of the modern world" was Queen Elizabeth II's description of the Barbican Centre, which she opened on 3 March 1982.

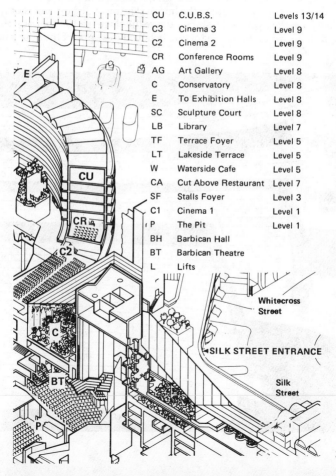

CU	C.U.B.S.	Levels 13/14
C3	Cinema 3	Level 9
C2	Cinema 2	Level 9
CR	Conference Rooms	Level 9
AG	Art Gallery	Level 8
C	Conservatory	Level 8
E	To Exhibition Halls	Level 8
SC	Sculpture Court	Level 8
LB	Library	Level 7
TF	Terrace Foyer	Level 5
LT	Lakeside Terrace	Level 5
W	Waterside Cafe	Level 5
CA	Cut Above Restaurant	Level 7
SF	Stalls Foyer	Level 3
C1	Cinema 1	Level 1
P	The Pit	Level 1
BH	Barbican Hall	
BT	Barbican Theatre	
L	Lifts	

Whitecross Street

◄SILK STREET ENTRANCE

Silk Street

Barbican Theatre

The RSC is built around a core of Associate Artists (actors, directors and designers) who, by working together over long periods with shared ideas, aim to achieve a distinctive style. The Company was formed in 1960 under the leadership of Peter Hall at Stratford-upon-Avon and later that year it took over the Aldwych Theatre as its London headquarters, before its Barbican residency.

The 1166-seat auditorium consists of a raked stalls area and three circles which project forward above each other towards the stage. The stage lies in front of, rather than behind, an arch, and the acting area is the focal point of every seat in the house. The most distant seat is only 65 feet from the front of the stage. Above the stage is a 109-foot double height flytower for scenery storage, believed to be one of the tallest in the world.

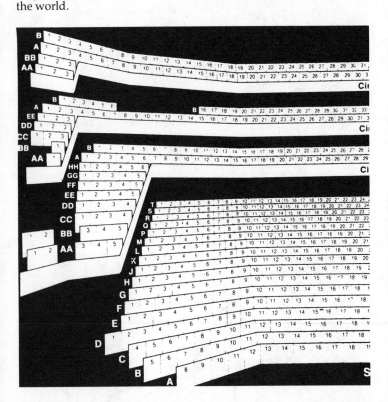

Barbican – The Pit

Complementing the Company's main-stage productions in the Barbican Theatre, the Royal Shakespeare Company presents small-scale productions of Shakespeare, revivals and new plays in The Pit.

Originally intended as a rehearsal room, The Pit has been adapted to form a flexible auditorium seating around 200 people on three of four sides of the acting area, depending on the design of individual productions. It has no set seating plan.

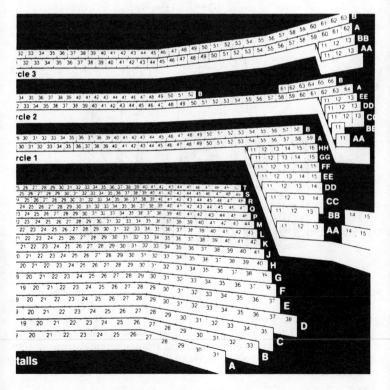

Cambridge Theatre

Earlham Street, WC2 9HU

Box Office: 10.00 to 20.00 hrs
Tel: 379 5299
Credit Cards: Yes
Underground: Covent Garden.

Bars: 3
Catering: Snacks
Seating: 1,273
Buses: 1, 14, 19, 22, 24, 29, 38, 176.

In 1930 when *The Cambridge* opened, there was another burst of theatre building going on in London. In the design of *The Cambridge* simplicity was, apparently, the keynote. *"The Stage"* of 4th September, 1930 remarked ". . . The beautiful, if somewhat peculiar decorative scheme appears to be Teutonic, and is strangely reminiscent of the then strange futuristic sets in German films immediately after the war of 1914-1918 . . ."

AUDITORIUM PLAN

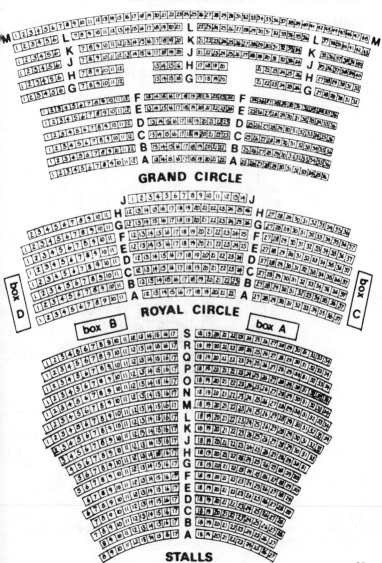

GRAND CIRCLE

ROYAL CIRCLE

box D

box C

box B

box A

STALLS

Comedy Theatre

Panton Street, SW1Y 4DN

Box Office: 10.00 to 20.00 hrs   Bars: 3
Tel: 867 1045   Seating: 780
Credit Cards: 836 3161
Underground: Piccadilly Circus. Buses: 1, 3, 6, 9, 12, 13, 14, 15, 19, 22, 38, 39, 53, 59, 88, 159, 505, 506.

The architect of *The Comedy* was Thomas Verity – who had the distinction of being one of the first English architects to design in a true French manner. (The French influence on theatre design, especially, was to continue into the early part of the 20th century.) Of his *Comedy Theatre*, *"The Era"* of 15th October, 1881 remarked ". . . It is Renaissance style richly moulded and finished in white and gold . . ."

Although electric light was to have been installed (as in *The Savoy*, which opened a few days before), the conventional gas system eventually prevailed. In less well-designed auditoria of this period the oxygen-consuming gas burners, together with overcrowding, made conditions extremely uncomfortable.

AUDITORIUM PLAN

BALCONY

ROYAL CIRCLE

DRESS CIRCLE

STALLS

Criterion Theatre

Piccadilly Circus, W1V 9LB

Box Office: 10.00 to 20.00 hrs
Tel: 867 1117
Credit Card Booking:
9.00-20.00 887 1111

Bars: 2
Catering: Coffee
Seating: 603

Underground: Piccadilly Circus. Buses: 3, 6, 9, 12, 13, 14, 15, 19, 22, 25, 38, 39, 53, 59, 88, 159.

In 1873 Spiers and Pond constructed a large restaurant, the Criterion, overlooking Piccadilly Circus, then known as Regent Circus. In the initial plans a small concert hall was to be incorporated in the middle of the building – however, during the construction, it was decided instead to convert it into a theatre. But this was to be no ordinary theatre for the designer, Thomas Verity, decided that it should be underground and even the upper circle had to be reached by descending stairs. In 1874 the idea was something of a novelty, ". . .

an underground Temple of Drama into which it was necessary to pump air to save the audience from being asphyxiated . . ."

One of the most delightful features of this charming little theatre is the beautifully preserved Victorian tile work and wall decorations. The auditorium which is pink, beige, soft and warm, manages to combine a quiet elegance with a cosy intimacy – qualities special to so many of the smaller London theatres.

AUDITORIUM PLAN

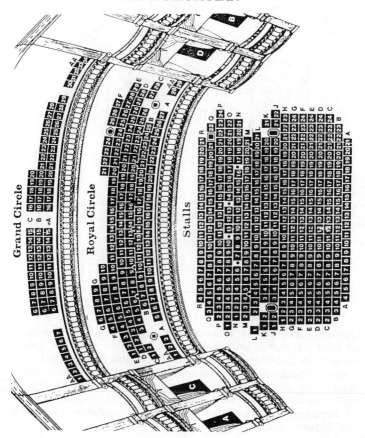

Dominion Theatre

Tottenham Court Road, W1P 0AG

Box Office: 10.00 to 20.00 hrs   Bars: 4 plus Function Suites
Tel: 580 9562/580 8845   Seating: 2,000
Credit Cards: Yes
Underground: Tottenham Court Road. Buses: 1, 7, 8, 14, 22, 24, 25, 29, 38, 55, 73, 134, 176.

Opened in 1929 on site of an old brewery, the mode of decoration adopted was that of the late French Renaissance. This vast theatre opened when movies where very much in vogue and became host to some spectacular films. The Sound of Music and South Pacific ran for many years. Since the 1970's, a mixed policy of cinema and theatre has been adopted. The Welsh National Opera make regular visits and it is hoped more major musicals will grace its stage after "Time" with Cliff Richard ran for two years.

AUDITORIUM PLAN

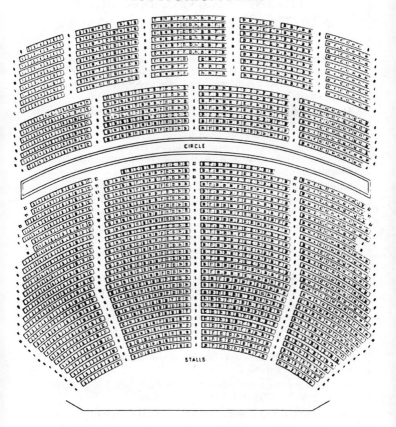

THE NATIONAL MUSEUM OF THE PERFORMING ARTS

The Theatre Museum is Britain's National Museum of the Performing Arts, and a branch of the Victoria and Albert Museum. It covers live forms of entertainment such as theatre, ballet, dance, opera, musical theatre, circus, magic, rock and pop.

The collections of over two million objects are among the largest and most important of their kind in the world. They include costumes, paintings, photographs, prints, drawings and designs, playbills, programmes, prompt books, props and puppets. Treasures range from actual theatre boxes rescued from Glasgow's Palace Theatre of Varieties to Mick Jagger's jumpsuit.

Within ten minutes' walk of over 30 theatres, the Theatre Museum presents different events during the year and stages a variety of special exhibitions on the performing arts in addition to the permanent displays.

The museum's box office sells tickets for West End shows, concerts, the Barbican, the National Theatre, and its own Studio Theatre where professional productions, workshops, illustrated talks and films take place.

Access to the research collections for scholars and researchers is free by appointment, and there is also a lively educational programme.

A shop selling posters, postcards and other theatrical gifts is on the ground floor and the cafe offers light refreshments and makes an ideal meeting place. A series of ramps makes all areas of the museum accessible for wheelchairs.

Gallery opening times: 11am - 7pm Tuesday to Sundays. Last ticket 6.30pm. Closed Mondays.

Box Office opening times: 11am - 8pm Tuesday to Saturdays (Sunday 11am - 7pm). Tel. (071) 836 2330. Closed Mondays.

Main Entrance: Russell Street, Covent Garden, London WC2.

Nearest underground: Covent Garden. BR: Waterloo and Charing Cross. Bus: 1, 4, 6, 9, 11, 13, 15, 24, 29, 55, 68, 77A, 170, 171, 172, 176, 188, 502 and 513 (to Aldwych or Strand).

Postal Address: 1E Tavistock Street, London WC2E 7PA. **Tel. No:** (071) 836 7891.

Donmar Theatre

41 Earlham Street, WC2H 9LD

Box Office Tel: 240 8230
Credit Card Booking: 379 6433/
379 6565
Bars: 1
Catering: Snacks
Seating: 240
Underground: Covent Garden. Buses: 1, 14, 19, 22, 24, 29, 38, 176.

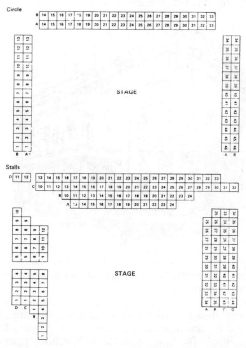

It's easy to pass by *The Warehouse* – in *The Donmar Theatre* in the heart of Covent Garden – without noticing it. You will see no bright lights or grand foyer for this is theatre in the raw! Operated by Omega Projects Ltd. A non-profit registered charity company.

The auditorium is simple – literally a warehouse with seats arranged around the stage area giving it an air of informality. Seats between 200 and 250.

Drury Lane Theatre

Catherine Street, WC2B 5JF

Box Office: 10.00 to 20.00 hrs   **Bars: 6**
Tel: 836 8108   **Catering: Snacks**
Credit Cards: Yes   **Seating: 2,245**
Underground: Covent Garden, Aldwych. Buses: 1, 4, 6, 9, 11, 13, 15, 55, 68, 77, 170, 171, 172, 188, 239, 501.

If such a shrine were to be dedicated then *Drury Lane* would surely become a High Altar of the Theatre, for probably nowhere else is quite so richly encrusted with its lore.

Since Restoration times four theatres have been housed on the site of the present theatre. Two were destroyed by fire, one was demolished and the fourth remains. It would take volumes to describe the sheer glory of *'The Lane'* with its architecture, paintings and statuary. Because the theatre has always been a mirror of fashion, styles have changed constantly, being influenced by grandoise continental themes, heavy Victoriana, Baroque flourishes and Edwardian imperialism. All are now intrinsically bound together by time, creating an atmosphere that is sometimes awesome, yet always welcoming.

The Patent and Charter of Old Drury (a copy of which is on view)

Drury Lane

was granted on 25th April, 1662 by King Charles II to Thomas Killigrew.

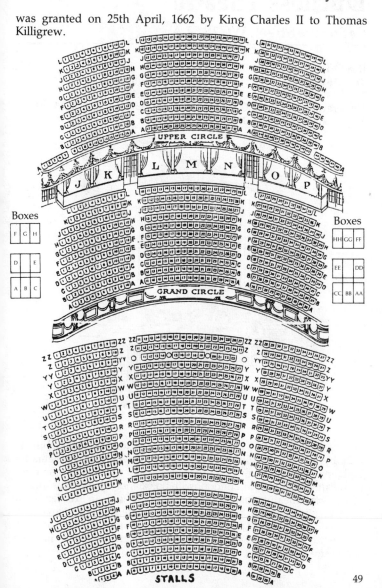

UPPER CIRCLE

Boxes

GRAND CIRCLE

Boxes

STALLS

Duchess Theatre

Catherine Street, WC2B 5LA

Box Office: 10.00 to 20.00 hrs   Bars: 2
Tel: 836 8243   Catering: No
Credit Cards: Yes   Seating: 476
Underground: Covent Garden, Aldwych. Buses: 1, 4, 6, 9, 11, 13, 15, 55, 68, 77, 170, 171, 172, 188, 239, 501.

One of the smaller and most comfortable theatres in London, built in 1929 by Ewan Barr, and despite numerous technical problems for both architect and engineers, the construction resulted in one of the best planned theatres in London, with an exterior described as *Modern Tudor Gothic*. Seating just under five hundred, with an excellent view from practically every seat, *The Duchess* opened on 25th November 1929 with a war play *'Tunnel Trench'*, and a young Emlyn Williams in the cast, who was later to return within six years and star in his own successful play *'Night Must Fall'*.

Duchess

Today, advanced lighting techniques and a fully equipped cinema projection unit give *The Duchess* a versatility to match the imagination of any director!

J.B. Priestley, as author of "Laburnum Grove", came to the theatre in 1933 and soon after started his long association with the management in which time two more of his plays were produced. His wife Mary Wyndham Lewis redesigned the interior in 1934 at which time a manifesto mentioned that ". . . Mr. Maurice Lambert, the brilliant sculptor, was commissioned to design and execute two great panels, in low bas-relief, for the niches between the proscenium and the dress circle . . . Patrons can see for themselves how well he triumphed and universal admiration has been expressed for his designs of figures holding conventional masks above applauding hands . . ."

AUDITORIUM PLAN

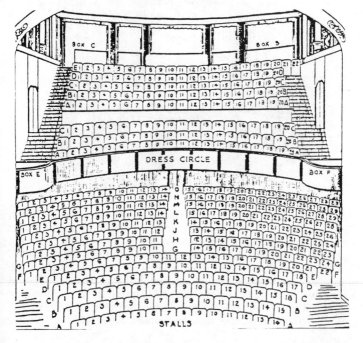

Duke of York's Theatre

St. Martin's Lane, WC2N 4BG

Box Office: 10.00 to 20.00 hrs
Tel: 836 5122/3
Credit Cards: Yes
Underground: Leicester Square. Buses: 1, 24, 29, 176.

Bars: 2
Catering: Coffee
Seating: 650

The Duke of York's Theatre was opened on 10th September 1892 with 'The Wedding Eve'. Was built by Frank Wyatt and his wife Violet Melnotte. Initially called *The Trafalgar* in 1894 and in the following year became *The Duke of York's* in honour of the future King, George V. The theatre has a famous association with J.M. Barrie arising from the production of 'Peter Pan' which opened in this theatre in 1904, and was revived every Christmas until 1915. During the run of the play 'Clouds' in 1979, Capital Radio purchased the freehold of *The Duke of York's Theatre*. The theatre was then closed down in May 1979 for complete re-furbishment, including removal of a number of pillars from the auditorium, and the installation of a recording studio in the gallery. The theatre then re-opened on 28th February 1980 under the aegis of Capital Radio with the play 'Rose' starring Glenda Jackson.

AUDITORIUM PLAN

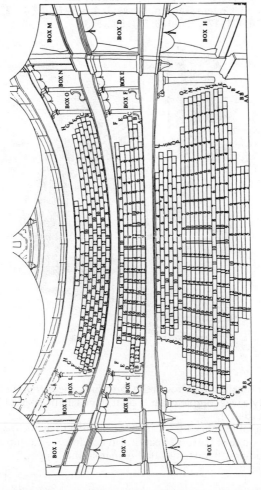

Fortune Theatre

Russell Street, WC2B 5HH (Covent Garden)

Box Office: 10.00 to 21.00 hrs   Bars: 2
Tel: 836 2238   Catering: Snacks
Credit Cards: Yes   Seating: 432
Underground: Covent Garden. Buses: 1, 4, 6, 9, 11, 13, 15, 22, 68, 77, 77A, 170, 171, 172, 176, 188, 501, 502, 513.

One of the smallest theatres in the West End, the *Fortune* built in the art deco style was completed in 1924. It stands in the heart of bustling Covent Garden.

'The Era' of October 1924 was of the opinion that "the theatre will certainly be one of the most beautiful in London . . . the entrance hall is an exceedingly handsome affair of marble and copper."

Fortune

Nowadays stages musicals, revues and plays, especially thrillers. *The Fortune* faces the famous colonnade of the Theatre Royal, Drury Lane, and is named after the original in the Barbican where Shakespeare performed.

AUDITORIUM PLAN

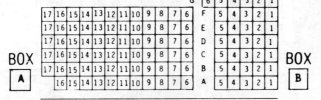

UPPER CIRCLE

DRESS CIRCLE

ORCHESTRA STALLS

Garrick Theatre

Charing Cross Road, WC2H 0HH

Box Office: 10.00 to 20.00 hrs   Bars: 2
Tel: 379 6107   Catering: No
Credit Cards: Yes   Seating: 675
Underground: Leicester Square. Buses: 1, 24, 29, 176.

In the late 1880s the reputation of the famous theatre architect Phipps was somewhat tarnished after his *Theatre Royal* at Exeter had burned down, causing the loss of some 140 lives. But, although his rival Walter Emden was officially chosen to design W.S. Gilbert's *Garrick Theatre*, Phipps, renowned for his 'clever planning under difficult conditions', was nevertheless consulted. And the conditions at *The Garrick* did indeed prove difficult – an underground river was discovered seeping into the foundations. At this point Gilbert apparently remarked that he couldn't decide whether to continue with the building or lease the fishing rights!

Garrick

Eventually, all the obstacles were overcome and the theatre duly opened on 24th April, 1889. *"The Era"* of 17th April noted that "... the auditorium is decorated in the Italian Renaissance style, the ornamental work being in high bold relief ... the box front of the dress circle tier is divided by groups of cupids supporting shields crowned with laurels, each shield bearing the name of a celebrated author ..."

The Garrick Theatre today is still heavy with the atmosphere of a Victorian playhouse. It is a richly elegant but friendly little theatre, built under a central dome, graced with magnificent chandeliers and, in the foyer, a copy of a Gainsborough portrait of the celebrated actor Garrick, the original having been lost. In true theatrical tradition there is also a ghost – reputedly that of Arthur Bourchier, a previous manager.

AUDITORIUM PLAN

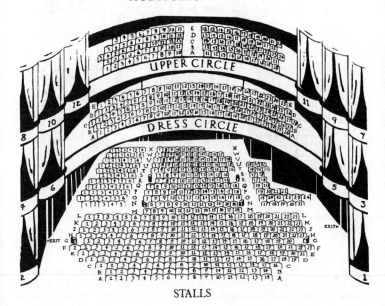

STALLS

Globe Theatre

Shaftesbury Avenue, W1V 7HB

Box Office: 10.00 to 21.00 hrs
Tel: 437 3667
Credit Cards: Yes
Underground: Piccadilly Circus.

Bars: 4
Catering: No
Seating: 983
Buses: 14, 19, 22, 38.

At the turn of the century a considerable number of new theatres were being built in and around London. The architect who was responsible for a great many of them, including most of the elegant little West End theatres which continue to delight, was W.G.R. Sprague.

Sprague was commissioned to design *The Hicks Theatre*, as it was first known, by a group including actor manager Seymour Hicks and Charles Fröhman, the American theatrical manager. The theatre was opened in 1906.

Globe

Sprague, like several other architects of his time, had a fondness for French themes. (It is interesting to note here that it was Sprague who, in fact, designed *The Edward VII Theatre* in Paris). And, of course, the Monarch's own affection for France possibly had some effect on the fashion of the day. In any event, much of the decorative style of *The Globe* is in the manner of Louis XVI although it must be said that the overall picture also relies on Baroque and Georgian influences.

AUDITORIUM PLAN

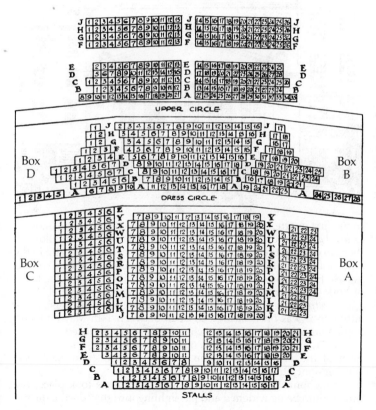

Haymarket, Theatre Royal

Haymarket, SW1Y 4HT

Box Office: 10.00 to 20.00 hrs
Tel: 930 9832
Credit Cards: Yes

Bars: 4
Catering: Sandwiches & Coffee
Seating: 906

Underground: Piccadilly Circus, Charing Cross. Buses: 6, 9, 12, 13, 14, 15, 19, 22, 25, 38, 39, 53, 59, 88, 159.

In the first quarter of the 18th century, only two theatres in London – *Drury Lane* and *Covent Garden*, held the necessary Patent allowing them to open to the public. For many years the "Little Theatre in the Hay" fought the legislation and put on entertainment under various guises. Finally, however, the Patent was obtained through the Duke of York – brother of King George III – and granted to Samuel Foote. *The Theatre Royal* (as it became) was then officially in business – although it was only allowed to open between 14th May and 14th September when the other two charter houses were closed.

In 1821, at a time when much of London was being restyled at the wish of the Prince Regent, the famous architect John Nash was commissioned to redesign the theatre.

Throughout the 19th century various alterations took place, the proscenium being widened and gas lighting introduced – the theatre

Haymarket

was, in fact, the last to be lit by candles. Around 1879, the eminent architect Phipps exerted a French influence when he attempted to emulate the interior of Victor Louis' *Grand Théâtre* de Bordeaux. Today, the auditorium with its ornate decor, gilding and ceiling paintings, remains gracious, elegant and decidedly regal.

AUDITORIUM PLAN

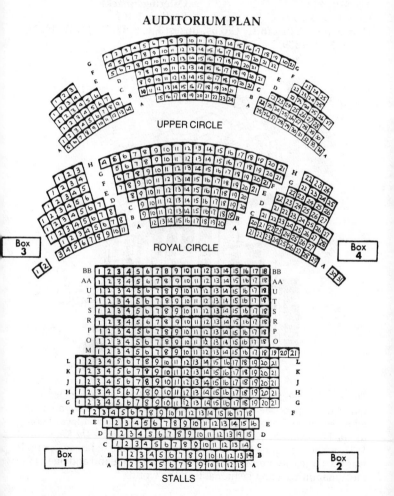

Her Majesty's Theatre

Haymarket, SW1Y 4QL

Box Office: 10.00 to 20.00 hrs   **Bars: 4**
Tel: 839 2244   **Catering: Snacks**
Credit Cards: Yes   **Seating: 1,161**
Underground: Piccadilly Circus. Buses: 3, 6, 9, 12, 13, 14, 15, 19, 22,
38, 53, 59, 88, 159.

The site of *Her Majesty's* has had theatrical association since 1705, when the first of the four theatres was built by Sir John Vanbrugh, who described the location as being ". . . the second stableyard going up the Hay-Market . . ." The second theatre, known as *The King's* until 1837, when it became *Her Majesty's*, was the home of Italian opera. It was the largest and most expensive theatre in England and one of the most magnificent and fashionable in the world.

Her Majesty's

The present theatre, built by the famous actor manager Beerbohm Tree, opened in 1897. A contemporary manifesto stated that ". . . the style, adopted for the auditorium of the theatre is Louis XVI. There are private boxes on each of the tiers adjoining the proscenium and separated from it and other parts of the auditorium by marble columns . . . The whole of the theatre and annexes are lighted by Electric Light . . . Hanging from the ceiling is a cut glass and brass electrolier . . ." Because of its exceptionally good acoustics, the theatre today is as popular with actors as with audiences. Outside, there still stands the arcade which was designed by Nash and Repton and completed in 1818 – while inside, the predominantly red auditorium with its large stage and fine ceiling paintings, remains as resplendent and dignified as ever.

AUDITORIUM PLAN

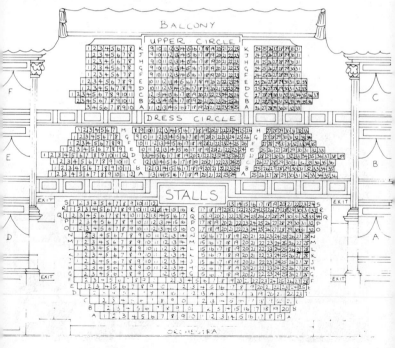

River Thames circa 1640

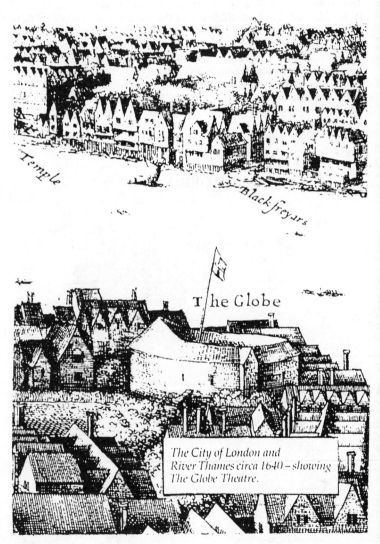

The City of London and
River Thames circa 1640 – showing
The Globe Theatre.

London Coliseum

Home of
English National Opera

St. Martin's Lane, WC2N 4ES

Box Office: 10.00 to 21.00 hrs
Tel: 836 3161
Credit Cards: 240 5258

Bars: 5
Catering: Sandwiches & Salads
Seating: 2,358

Limited accommodation for the disabled is available at reduced prices in the stalls boxes. Please telephone for full details.
Underground: Leicester Square, Charing Cross. Buses: 1, 3, 6, 9, 11, 12, 13, 15, 23, 24, 29, 53, 77, 77a, 88, 159, 170, 172, 176, all stop nearby.

An exquisite furnished mobile lounge, designed to transport Royal guests to their box, lifts to carry audiences to the upper parts of the theatre, foyer facilities for typing messages and sending telegrams . . . these were just a few of the innovations which impressed Londoners in 1904 when Oswald Stoll opened his *London Coliseum*.

As the name implies, the theatre was designed on Romanesque lines. Grandoise and broad sweeping, complete with Roman chariots,

London Coliseum

granite columns and arches – the sheer splendour remains today. Yet despite the vastness there is a certain warmth and intimacy, typified perhaps in the unusual stalls – level boxes at the back of the auditorium. (There are, of course, conventional boxes at all other levels.)

The globe on the top of the building was designed to revolve but it was deemed illegal and Stoll was obliged to fix it in a stationary

AUDITORIUM PLAN

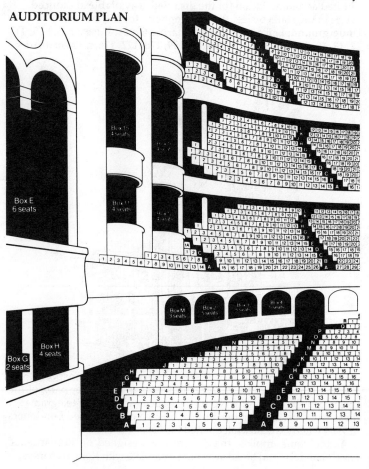

London Coliseum

position. However, he was able to incorporate flashing electric lights which gave the illusion of movement and this remains a famous feature of the London skyline. In the sixties Sadler's Wells Opera, now English National Opera, made *The Coliseum* their West End home.

International ballet companies also perform for short summer seasons.

The opera season runs from September to June.

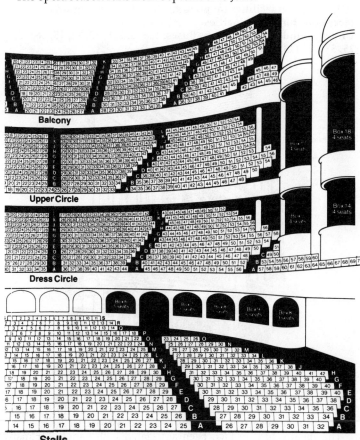

Balcony

Upper Circle

Dress Circle

Stalls

London Palladium Theatre

Argyll Street, W1A 3AB

Box Office: 10.00 to 20.00 hrs
Tel: 437 7373/437 2055
Credit Cards: Yes

Bars: 5
Catering: Snacks
Seating: 2,317

VIP Reception facilities for up to 40 after show and mid-day receptions for private parties.
Underground: Oxford Circus. Buses: 1, 3, 6, 7, 8, 12, 13, 15, 16, 23, 25, 53, 73, 113, 159, 500.

On Sunday evenings in the sixties Britain switched on to "Sunday Night At The London Palladium" – the variety show which became almost as much of an institution as the Sunday roast itself!

The theatre has, in fact, been associated with variety for many years, while the site on which it is built has been connected with entertainment for over a century.

London Palladium

In 1871, Frederick Hengler acquired a lease on the original property and staged his successful "Hengler's Grand Cirque" – eventually being superseded by the *National Skating Palace*. Efforts were later made to resurrect the circus, but by then the Public's imagination had been caught by the more breathtaking spectaculars as the new *London Hippodrome*.

AUDITORIUM PLAN

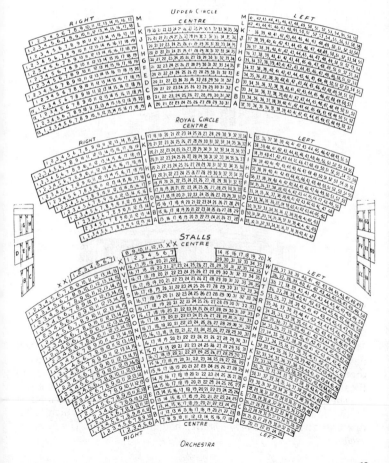

Lyric Theatre

Shaftesbury Avenue, W1V 8ES

Box Office: 10.00 to 20.00 hrs   Bars: 3
Tel: 437 3686   Catering: Snacks
Credit Cards: Yes   Seating: 948
Underground: Piccadilly Circus. Buses: 14, 19, 22, 38.

The last years of the 19th century saw great activity in the fast developing areas around the new Shaftesbury Avenue. Undoubtedly there were fortunes to be made and one man who had the key to theatreland success was Henry J. Leslie, builder of *The Lyric Theatre*.

When everyone else was losing heart, Leslie purchased an interest in the initially unsuccessful comic opera "Dorothy" which, after opening at the old *Gaiety Theatre*, had transferred to *The Prince of Wales*.

Leslie effected a few changes and soon "Dorothy" started to flourish. He then decided to transfer the show to his own new theatre when it opened, reputedly ending up with a tidy £100,000 profit in his pocket!

In 1933 Michael Rosenauer completely refurbished the theatre leaving on it the unmistakeable stamp of the thirties.

AUDITORIUM PLAN

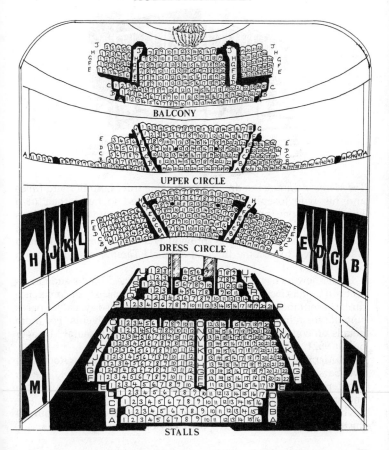

Mermaid Theatre

Puddledock, Blackfriars, EC4V 3DB

Box Office: 10.00 to 20.30 hrs
Tel: 410 0000
Credit Cards: Yes
Parking: NCP nearby.
Underground: Blackfriars. Buses: 45, 59, 63, 76, 141, 184.

Bars: 3
Catering: Servery
Seating: 604

The Mermaid Theatre is a dream which came true. Lord Bernard Miles and his wife Josephine had always wanted to build their own Elizabethan-style theatre, and in 1945, when they moved to St. John's Wood, the seed was already sown. There, in their own back garden, was a large wooden building (previously a school classroom) which was destined to become the first *Mermaid Theatre*, opening on 9th September, 1951.

Under new management since 1983, *The Mermaid Theatre* auditorium seats 610, offers facilities for the disabled and is available for conference hire, presentations, seminars and trade shows. Also available spaces suitable for rehearsals, lectures and other smaller events. For more details on conference facilities, please contact the General Manager on 236 9521.

The Mermaid also houses a Self Service Restaurant, River Room and two bars. The Servery has a wide range of hot and cold meals, vegetarian dishes and a selection of salads and is open from 12-3pm and for pre-theatre meals.

The River Room offers original cocktails with a theatrical flavour, all the traditional beverages, and above all a glorious view of the Thames.

AUDITORIUM PLAN

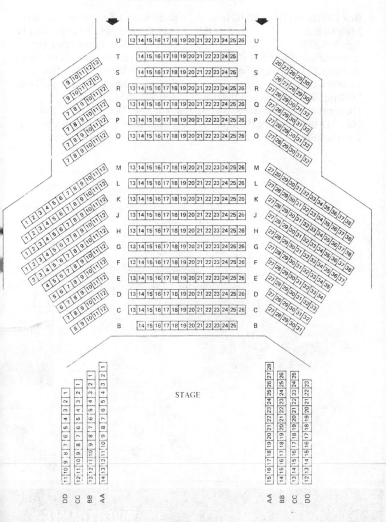

National Theatre

South Bank, SE1 9PX

Box Office: 10.00 to 20.00 hrs
Mon to Sat.
Tel: 928 2252
Information Line: 633 0880
10.00 to 23.00 Mon to Sat.
Credit Cards: Yes
Seating: see text for each theatre

Buffets and Bars: Espresso Bar
(not shown) 8am-3.30pm Mon-Fri
8am-6pm Sat; 10am-5pm Sun.
Catering: restaurant – Ovations:
lunch - 12.15pm, last orders 2pm;
dinner - 5.30pm, last orders 11pm.
Tel: 928 2033 ext 561.

Underground: Waterloo. Buses: 1, 4, 68, X68, 168, 171, 176, 188, 501,
502, 513 to Waterloo Bridge; 70, 70A, 76 to Stamford Street close by.
Car Park: 8am-2am except Sunday – spaces only £2 after 5pm.

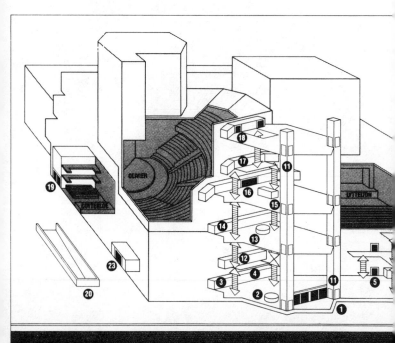

National Theatre

The National Theatre is a great building in every sense. Architect Sir Denys Lasdun incorporated not only **three auditoriums** but **eight bars** and a **restaurant** plus modern workshops, paint rooms, wardrobes, property shops, rehearsal rooms and advanced technical facilities, the like of which had never been seen in a British theatre – where backstage, cramped and difficult conditions were all too often the norm.

The original concepts for Britain's *National Theatre* started by the late Lord Olivier, continued by its second Director Sir Peter Hall, remain the goals of its current Director Richard Eyre and Executive Director David Aukin. The building on London's South Bank now stands a lasting reminder of the vision of its founding Director Lord Olivier, and all who work in it and visit it are reminded of his enormous contribution to the theatre in Britain and in particular the Royal *National Theatre*.

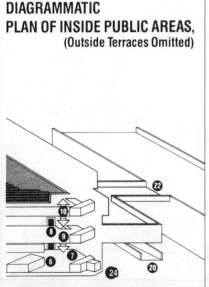

DIAGRAMMATIC PLAN OF INSIDE PUBLIC AREAS, (Outside Terraces Omitted)

PLAN OF INSIDE PUBLIC AREAS
(Outside Terraces Omitted)

1. Main entrance
2. Lyttelton information desk
3. Lyttelton cloakroom
4. Box office
5. Lyttelton stalls bar
6. Main bookshop
7. Lyttelton buffet
8. Lyttelton circle (main exhibition area)
9. Lyttelton circle bar
10. Terrace cafe
11. Lifts to Olivier
12. Ovations – The National's Restaurant and Wine Bar
13. Olivier information desk
14. Olivier cloakroom
15. Olivier bookstall
16. Olivier stalls entrance (bars left and right)
17. Olivier buffet
18. Olivier circle entrance gallery (exhibition area)
19. Cottesloe Theatre entrance
20. Underground car park entrances
21. Disabled car parking spaces
22. Exit to Waterloo Bridge via terrace
23. Stage door
24. Espresso bar

 Staircases

National Theatre/Olivier

There are daily conducted tours of the building (except Sunday) including the workshops and backstage areas. Walk through this amazing complex and, in addition to theatregoers of all ages, you will see visitors and Londoners alike strolling through the spacious foyers; meeting friends; enjoying a drink or a meal; browsing through bookstalls; listening to impromptu music in the foyers; or simply standing on one of the terraces and marvelling at the continuous pageant of craft flowing past the magnificent backdrop of the City on the other side of the water.

Each of Lasdun's theatres is totally different in design and adaptable enough to meet all kinds of dramatic requirements, thus offering enormous scope for both directors and actors. For audiences, too, *The National Theatre* promotes new levels of discovery and enjoyment. The designers have, quite literally, set the stages for much closer communication between actor and audience. Acoustics and sight

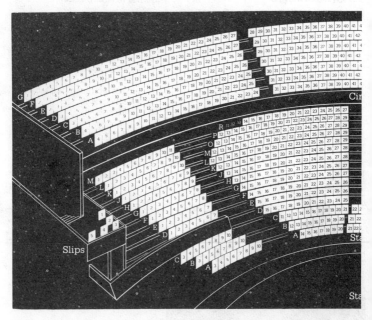

lines in all three theatres are first class, ensuring that every seat is a good one and, incidentally, a reasonably priced one. A high proportion of seats are offered daily at considerably less than one would expect to pay at most West End theatres. The modern facilities at *The National Theatre* also mean that it is easier to cater for a constantly changing repertoire, guaranteeing that at least once a month most tastes can be accommodated!

The theatre, named after actor Sir Laurence Olivier, who was also the first Director of *The National* during its years at *The Old Vic*, is the centre of the complex. It can accommodate 1,160 people in its fan-shaped auditorium and dispenses with the conventional proscenium arch and safety curtain. *The Olivier* can serve dramatics of every period and theatre of every sort, and in spite of its size, has a concentrated intimacy. No seat is far from the actor's point of command and the seats match his effective span of vision, thus adding a new relationship between actor and audience.

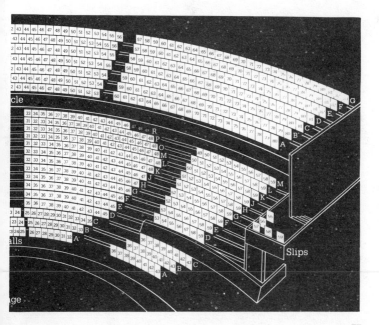

National Theatre/Cottesloe

The Cottesloe is the smallest, barest and most flexible of *The National Theatre* houses. It is a dark-walled rectangular space capable of accommodating up to 400 people if necessary. The seating can be removed and the stage can be used in any way, for any kind of production, from classical staging to experimental theatre.

On three sides of the room are two tiers of pillared galleries – reminiscent of the inn yards which preceded Shakespearean stages. The theatre is named after Lord Cottesloe, chairman of the South Bank Board (the body for the construction of *The National Theatre*) and a former Chairman of the Arts Council. (No set seating plan).

AUDITORIUM PLAN

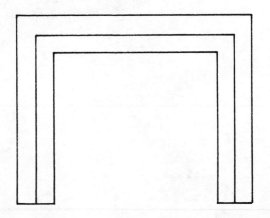

National Theatre/Lyttleton

The Lyttleton is a proscenium theatre which can hold 890 people. As elsewhere in *The National Theatre* the walls are roughly-finished shuttered concrete to promote efficient acoustics. The proscenium is adaptable and it is possible to make an open end-stage effect, while a down-stage lift can create a fore-stage or an orchestra pit for up to 20 musicians.

Complete sets can also be prepared behind soundproof doors ready to slide onto the stage. The theatre is named after Oliver Lyttleton, Viscount Chandos, whose parents were among the earlist campaigners for *The National Theatre* and who was himself its first Chairman from 1962 to 1971.

AUDITORIUM PLAN

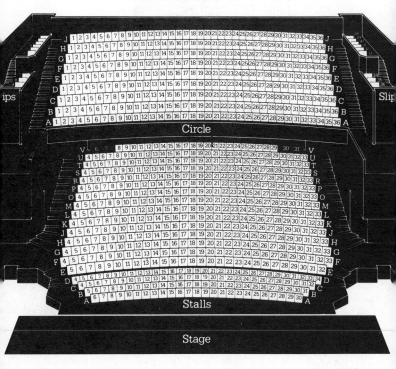

79

New London Theatre

Parker Street, Drury Lane, WC2B 5PW

Box Office: 10.00 to 19.45 hrs
Tel: 405 0072

Bars: 2
Catering: By arrangement
Seating: 1,106

Underground: Covent Garden, Holborn. **Buses:** 1, 8, 14, 19, 22, 24, 25, 29, 38, 73, 176.

The New London Theatre, which has been both a conventional theatre and a conference centre in its time.

The site of *The New London* at 167 Drury Lane has held licensed premises since the reign of Elizabeth I. Nell Gwynn, who lived nearby, was associated with the Mogul Tavern of the 17th century, which eventually developed into the Music Hall known to Londoners as "Old Mo".

New London

"... *The New London* is a theatre of the future. It is a theatre that moves: stage, seats, lights – even the walls can be made to change position . . ." It is indeed an extremely versatile theatre and can adopt from 'proscenium to 'theatre-in-the-round' literally at the flick of a switch. Despite its historical foundations, *The New London* is ultra modern in design with a spacious brown and beige auditorium, behind which is the 2,400 square foot foyer with its large glass window, bars and comfortable lounge areas. CATS has been running since May 81. It is now the longest running British Musical as of May 12 1989.

AUDITORIUM PLAN

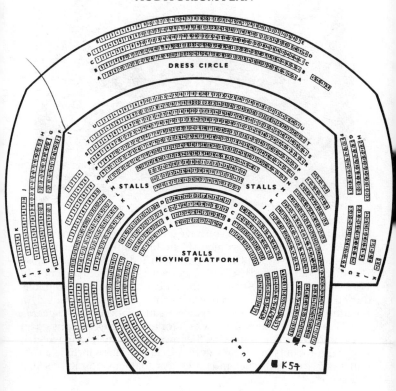

Open Air Theatre

Inner Circle, Regent's Park, NW1 4NP

Box Office: 10.00 to 20.00 hrs during season: June, July, August, May 10.00 to 17.00 hrs
Tel: 486 2431
Credit Cards: Yes
Bars: 1
Underground: Baker Street. Buses: 2, 2B, 13, 18, 27, 30, 74, 82, 113, 159.

Catering: Cold buffet and Barbecue. Inclusive price (ticket and food) for parties only by prior arrangement. Picknickers welcome.
Seating: 1,187 plus 60 on grass

Take a delightful woodland setting, a gentle summer's evening and a fine company of players and you have the magic ingredients which go to make a visit to London's unique *Open Air Theatre* so enjoyable. The idea of staging plays in the park was initiated by Ben Greet whose Woodland Players used to entertain audiences in Edwardian times. In 1932, Sydney Carroll resurrected the tradition, with a few exceptions during the war years. Three productions are now presented in repertory each summer, two of which are the works of Shakespeare.

1975 saw the opening of a new auditorium complex comprising an upper and lower tier – replacing the rows of deck chairs and wooden seats with room beneath for catering facilities. These include a cold buffet service, barbecue and large bar, famous for its cocktail specialities.

AUDITORIUM PLAN

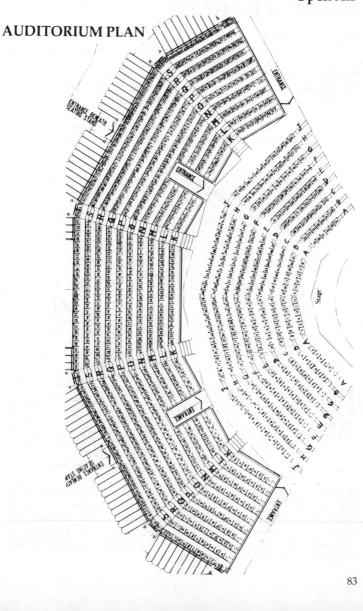

Palace Theatre

Shaftesbury Avenue, W1A 4AF

Box Office: 10.00 to 20.00 hrs
Tel: 434 0909
Credit Cards: Yes

Bars: 5
Catering: Snacks. Lunchtime Restaurant.
Seating: 1,480
Cloakroom: Attendant

Underground: Leicester Square. Buses: 1, 14, 19, 22, 24, 29, 38, 176.

The Royal English Opera House (as *The Palace* was first known) opened its doors on 31st January, 1891 with "Ivanhoe", a romantic opera by Arthur Sullivan. English audiences, however, failed to support this and the several other offerings which swiftly followed, and Richard D'Oyly Carte's dream of an English Opera House finally faded in 1892 when the theatre became *The Palace of Varieties*.

AUDITORIUM PLAN

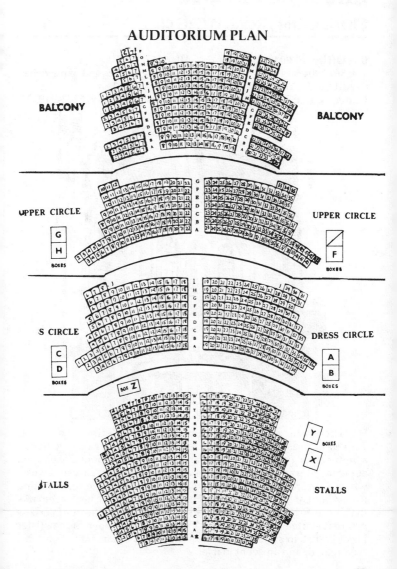

BALCONY

BALCONY

UPPER CIRCLE

UPPER CIRCLE

G
H
BOXES

F
BOXES

S CIRCLE

DRESS CIRCLE

C
D
BOXES

A
B
BOXES

BOX Z

STALLS

STALLS

Y BOXES

X

Phoenix Theatre

Charing Cross Road, WC2H 0JP

Box Office: 10.00 to 20.00 hrs
Tel: 867 1004/5
Credit Cards: Yes
Bars: 5
Catering: Coffee and Sandwiches
Seating: 1,012
Underground: Tottenham Court Road. Buses: 1, 14, 19, 22, 24, 29, 38, 55, 176.

For 'The Master', Noel Coward and his beloved Gertrude Lawrence, *The Phoenix* was to be 'their' theatre in which they starred together on a number of occasions in Coward's own productions. Their first appearance was on the theatre's opening night in "Private Lives", which Coward had written in about four days while recuperating from a bout of 'flu' in Shanghai. His biographer, Cole Lesley remarks that ". . . 'Private Lives' was deck'd in a glorious sheen of success before it started and in addition it was chosen to open Sidney (later Lord) Bernstein's *Phoenix Theatre*, a smart new ornament to London's theatreland, and an event in itself . . ."

Phoenix Theatre

Although it has been redecorated since, the theatre with its wood panelling, red seating and elegant chandelier, retains that delightfully intimate and stylish atmosphere typical of such theatres of the thirties. In 1969, Noel Coward opened the bar which is named after him. In another of the theatre's bars are some famous Punch cartoonists' original interpretations of a theme of 'the rising of the Phoenix'.

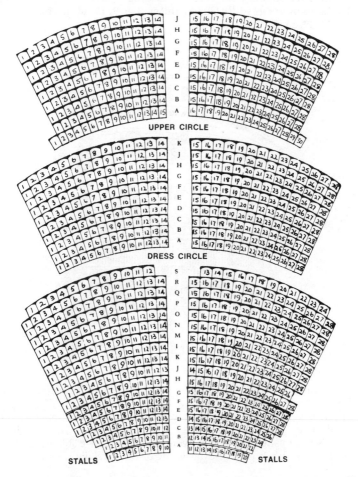

UPPER CIRCLE

DRESS CIRCLE

STALLS

STALLS

Piccadilly Theatre

Denman Street, W1V 8DY

Box Office: 10.00 to 20.00 hrs
Tel: 867 1118
Credit Card Booking: 867 1111
Underground: Piccadilly Circus. Buses: 3, 6, 9, 13, 14, 15, 19, 22, 25, 38, 39, 53, 88, 159.

Bars: 4
Catering: Buffet
Seating: 1,232

Victorian and Edwardian times, the heydays of British threatre building, inevitably nurtured a certain breed of architect who specialised in theatre design – Frank Matcham, William Sprague and Bertie Crewe, to name but a few. Although this golden age had largely diminished by the late twenties, Bertie Crewe still brought all his flair and expertise to the designing of *The Piccadilly Theatre*.

Piccadilly

The area chosen for impersario Edward Laurillard's new theatre was covered by run-down stables but by 1928 they had been replaced by a handsome building of white Portland stone. The original interior design was carried out by Marc-Henri but has since been altered, the modern amenities now including air conditioning and well appointed bars.

AUDITORIUM PLAN

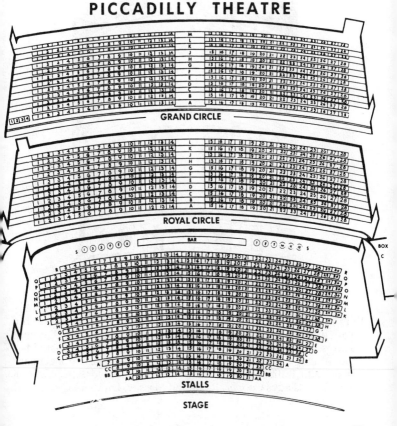

Playhouse Theatre

Northumberland Avenue, WC2N 5DE

Box Office: 10.00 to 20.00 hrs   Bars: 3
Tel: 839 4401   Catering: Shaw's Restaurant
Credit Cards: Yes   Seating: 790
Underground: Charing Cross, Embankment. Buses: 1, 3, 6, 9, 11, 12, 13, 15, 24, 29, 53, 77A, 77, 88, 109, 159, 170, 176, 184.

Built in 1882: now, more than 100 years later, it has been lavishly restored into one of the West End's most beautiful and charming theatres. This historic theatre has had an eventful and star-studded past. Among the actors who have graced its stage are legendary names of the British theatre such as Noel Coward, Ivor Novello, Sybil Thorndike, Gladys Cooper, Raymond Massey, Laurence Olivier and Alec Guinness.

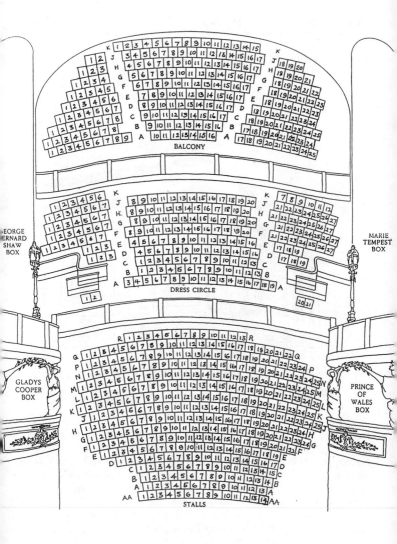

BALCONY

GEORGE BERNARD SHAW BOX

MARIE TEMPEST BOX

DRESS CIRCLE

GLADYS COOPER BOX

PRINCE OF WALES BOX

STALLS

Prince Edward Theatre

Old Compton Street, W1V 6HS

Box Office: 10.00 to 20.00 hrs
Tel: 734 8951
Credit Cards: Yes
Underground: Piccadilly Circus Tottenham Court Road. Buses: 1, 14, 19, 22, 24, 29, 38.

Bars: 4
Catering: No
Seating: 1,647

Designed by Edward A. Stone, *The Prince Edward* was the first of a spate of theatres to be constructed in the thirties. Within five years, however, it was converted into a cabaret-restaurant and at one point *The London Casino* (as it was now known), was reputed to be taking between £6,000 and £7,000 a week – more than any other place of entertainment in London! In 1946 it became a theatre once more – until 1954, when after suitable conversions, the big screen Cinerama arrived. In 1974, under Bernard Delfont's direction, the theatre was converted into a dual purpose film and theatre centre.

Prince Edward

In 1978 Andrew Lloyd Webber and Tim Rice's hit musical "Evita"
brought visitors and residents alike flocking to *The Prince Edward*.

AUDITORIUM PLAN

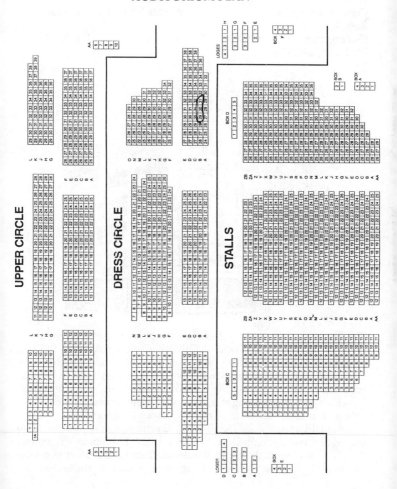

Prince of Wales Theatre

Coventry Street, W1V 8AS

Box Office: 10.00 to 20.00 hrs
Tel: 839 5972
Credit Cards: Yes
Bars: 4

Catering: No
Seating: 1,122
Private Room for 12 persons

Underground: Covent Garden, Embankment. Buses: 1, 6, 9, 11, 13, 15, 77, 170, 176.

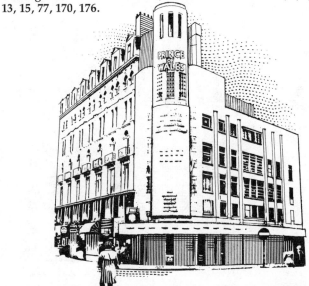

The Prince of Wales, now under the direction of Lord Delfont and a member of the now FIRST LEISURE CORPORATION PLC, is essentially a happy theatre, synonymous with good family entertainment and, of course, famous for its numerous television broadcasts. Walking into the spacious auditorium one can almost hear the spontaneous laughter and enthusiastic applause which have echoed round the rafter on so many glorious occasions.

Originally, known as *The Prince's*, the theatre was built by actor manager Edgar Bruce in 1884. *"The Era"* of the 12th January mentions that ". . . the general tone of the decorations is navy, white, cream colour and gold, the gliding being in large masses . . . the audience the stalls, after leaving the vestibule, descend by a spacious staircase through a foyer which is decorated and fitted up in the Moorish style and under the vestibule is a circular room, also in the Moorish style, for smoking, having a grotto constructed under the street . . ."

But in 1936 all that was to change. Robert Cromie redesigned *The Prince of Wales* (the name changed in 1886) in a style typical of the era – with sweeping curves and almost stark simplicity. And for anyone who has had to employ football scrum techniques in order to get a drink at some of the smaller theatre bars, there is good news – those at *The Prince of Wales* have been constructed on a grand scale!

AUDITORIUM PLAN

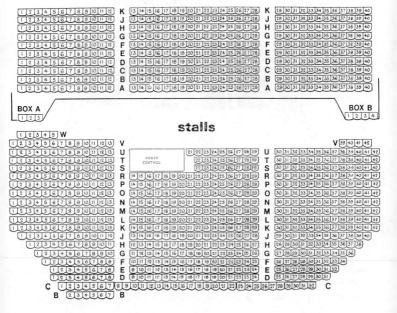

Queen's Theatre

Shaftesbury Avenue, W1V 8BA

Box Office: 10.00 to 20.00 hrs   Bars: 2
Tel: 734 1166   Catering: Coffee
Credit Cards: Yes   Seating: 979
Underground: Piccadilly Circus. Buses: 14, 19, 22, 38.

"He is after a knighthood" remarked George Bernard Shaw of his associate Vedrenne, "it is not for nothing that he called his theatre *The Queen's* . . . but why not The Alexandra?" In any event, on 8th October, 1907, Vedrenne's *Queen's Theatre* opened on the corner of Shaftesbury Avenue and Wardour Street.

The wind of change was undoubtedly blowing in all directions, emphasised further when Vedrenne announced that evening dress was to be optional in part of the dress circle. The style of the interior was elegant and handsome, borrowing a little from Italian, Georgian and Edwardian themes. Sadly, however, the foyer and rear of the circles suffered bomb damage and in the late fifties the theatre was reconstructed, though inside the original style was largely retained.

AUDITORIUM PLAN

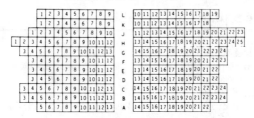

UPPER CIRCLE

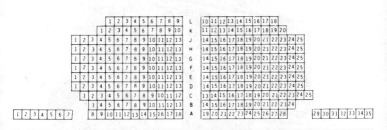

DRESS CIRCLE

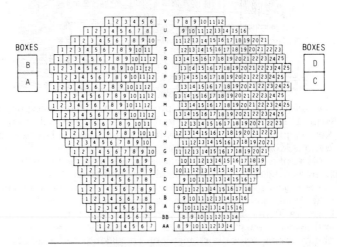

ORCHESTRA STALLS

Royal Court Theatre

Sloane Square, SW1W 3EE

Box Office: 10.00 to 20.00 hrs
Tel: Main House 730 1745
Theatre Upstairs 730 2554
Credit Cards: Yes
Underground: Sloane Square. Buses: 11, 19, 22, 219, C1

Bars: 2
Catering: Snacks
Seating: 395

The Royal Court is known for producing and commissioning new writing. The Press often refer to it as "Britain's National Theatre of New Writing'. Has received Best Play awards for the last two years 'Serious Money' and 'Our Country's Good'.

Many of today's leading dramatists made their debuts at *The Royal Court* as have numerous successful West End productions.

The Royal Court has origins dating back to 1870 when a dissenting chapel was converted into a theatre known at first as *The New Chelsea*. Local residents apparently regarded the transformation without enthusiasm, remarking that there were already actors, boxes, a pit, money-taking at the doors, histrionics of all kinds and incredibly bad acting!

Royal Court

Destined for a short run, *The New Chelsea* became *The Belgravia* and before the end of 1870 had been converted into ". . . a bright little theatre capable of seating comfortably 1,100 persons. It is gorgeous in gilding, profuse in ornamentation and its hangings and box curtains are of a pinkish mauve satin . . ." Thus run the description in *"The Illustrated London News"* of 4th February, 1871. The name was then changed to *The Royal Court*.

Following the theatre's closure and subsequent demolition, manager John Clayton built a new theatre (the present building) on the east side of the square which opened in September, 1888. After suffering bomb damage in 1940, the theatre remained derelict until Robert Cromie renovated it for the London Theatre Guild in 1952. More improvements followed with the arrival of the English Stage Company in 1956 and in 1971 the old rehearsal rooms became *The Theatre Upstairs*.

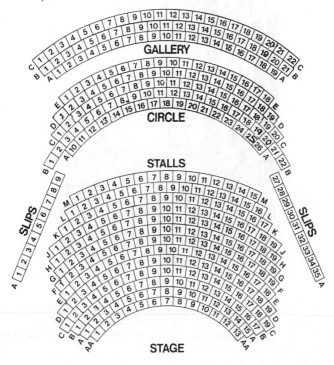

Royalty Theatre

Portugal Street, WC2A 2HT

Box Office: 10.00 to 20.00 hrs
Tel: 831 0660
Credit Cards: Yes

Bars: 2
Catering: Snacks
Seating: 1,037

Underground: Holborn, Aldwych. Buses: 1, 4, 6, 9, 11, 13, 15, 55, 68, 77, 170, 171, 172, 176, 188, 239, 501.

The Royalty Theatre of today is an exciting new concept, presenting a mixture of shows, concerts, conferences and a whole host of media events. There are extensive bar and reception facilities for these special occasions.

Royalty

The auditorium is spacious and comfortable and most attractive.

The Royalty is constructed on part of the ground which originally housed *The London Opera House*, later *The Stoll Theatre*, and opened in 1960 after Dame Edith Evans had unveiled the dedication stone. It was designed, as the press manifesto stated ". . . to combine the dignity of the Georgian threatre with the lushness of the Victorian theatre in present day terms . . ." *The Royalty* is a proscenium open stage theatre equipped with a lift which can rise to stage level.

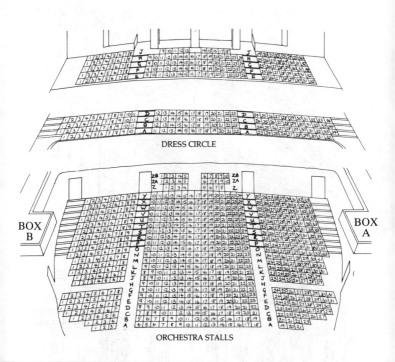

DRESS CIRCLE

BOX B

BOX A

ORCHESTRA STALLS

Royal Opera House

Covent Garden, WC2E 7QA

Box Office: 10.00 to 20.00 hrs
Tel: 240 1066
Credit Cards: Access, Amex, Visa, Diners Club

Bars: 9
Catering: 4 Buffet Bars
Seating: 2,156

Underground: Covent Garden. Buses: 1, 4, 6, 9, 11, 13, 15, 23, 68, 77, 170, 171, 172, 176, 188, 501, 502, 513.

Royal Opera House

For some people the name Covent Garden conjures up an image of the famous fruit and vegetable market, while for others it is *The Royal Opera House* – and, indeed, for 250 years they each went about their respective business side by side.

The first of the three theatres opened in 1732 and was one of the two London Theatres to hold a Patent permitting the performance of drama – the other being *The Theatre Royal*, Drury Lane. Apart from a few short seasons of Italian opera and an association with Handel, it was primarily devoted to drama – attracting to its stage such great names as David Garrick, Mrs. Siddons and the Kembles. However, on 19th September, 1808 it was burned down, taking with it Handel's organ and some manuscripts.

The second theatre, designed by Richard Smirke, was said to be the largest in Europe – Flaxman's bas-reliefs and statues, representing Comedy and Tragedy, have survived to this day and can now be seen behind the portico. Because of the vast cost of rebuilding, the new management attempted to raise the seat prices when the auditorium theatre opened in 1809, but this proved extremely unpopular and resulted in the famous 'Old Prices' Riots which lasted for 61 nights until the prices were reduced. In 1847 the theatre became *The Royal Italian Opera* but nine years later it too was destroyed by fire. Its replacement, which finally opened in 1858, was designed by Sir Edward Barry and remains today as sumptuous and magnificent as ever – with its great dome and fine Victorian auditorium, eminently regal in red, gold and cream. The chandelier has now been moved and many of the private boxes – which previously ran around all three tiers – have been opened up. However, the profile of the young Queen Victoria above the proscenium and the rows of cherubs which decorate the front of each tier (and reach a more advanced stage of womanhood at each descending level!) remain.

Some of the greatest names in the history of opera are associated with Covent Garden, including the legendary Patti, Nellie Melba, Caruso, Gobbi and Maria Callas. The late 19th and early 20th centuries saw the 'Golden Age' of the Opera House with extravagant Gala Performances – the Royal Box decked out in great glory and the programmes printed on white silk. This tradition was revived in 1977 with the Silver Jubilee Gala. Sir Thomas Beecham also played an important role in the theatre's development – although dedicated to opera, it was he who brought over Diaghilev's Russian Ballet and so started the ballet tradition. Since 1939 the theatre has been officially known as *the Royal Opera House* and in 1946 it became the national

Royal Opera House

home of both Opera and Ballet – the long list of the famous being joined by such celebrated names as Dame Ninette de Valois, Sir Frederick Ashton, Constant Lambert, Dame Margot Fonteyn,

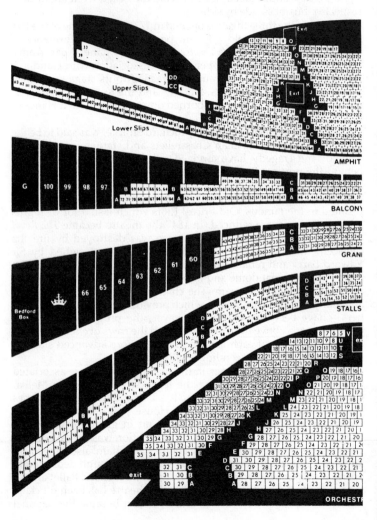

Rudolph Nureyev and many others. The Sadler's Wells Ballet became The Royal Ballet in 1956 and in October 1968, The Covent Garden Opera became The Royal Opera.

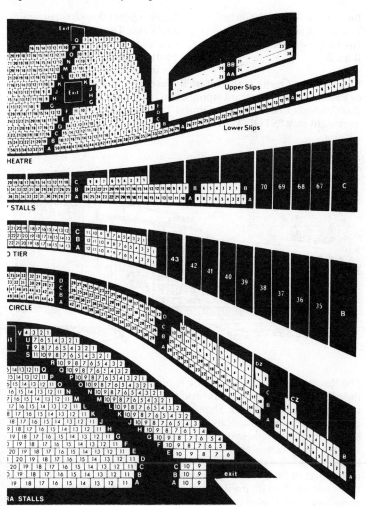

Royal Shakespeare Theatre

Stratford-upon-Avon, Warwickshire CV37 6BB

Box Office: 9.30 to 20.00 hrs
Tel: 0789 295623
Credit Cards: Yes
Bars: 3

Catering: Box Tree Restaurant
and River Terrace Restaurant.
Reservations tel: 0789 293226
Seating: RSC 1,500
Swan Theatre 450

Shakespeare Connection – InterCity fast train Euston to Coventry, or Paddington to Stratford-upon-Avon, change at Leamington Spa. Bus: Victoria Coach Station: Dinner/Theatre package with/without overnight stay "STOPOVER" 0789 414999.

The Royal Shakespeare Company is probably one of the best known theatre companies in the world and stages a varied repertoire ranging from new productions of Shakespeare's plays to plays by contemporary writers and musicals. It was not until 1769 that the idea of staging regular Shakespeare Festivals at his birthplace of Stratford was seriously considered and another century before a permanent Memorial was established. In 1986 the Swan Theatre opened – built inside part of the shell of the *Memorial Theatre* that survived the 1926 fire when the theatre itself was destroyed, leaving only the museum and connecting bridge unscathed.

Royal Shakespeare Theatre

The Swan Theatre stages mainly the work of Shakespeare's contemporaries whose work is now rarely performed. Theatre tours give a fascinating insight into the way the theatre works and runs most days (inc. Sundays).

The Other Place, the RSC's small intimate theatre is currently being rebuilt and is expected to open in 1991.

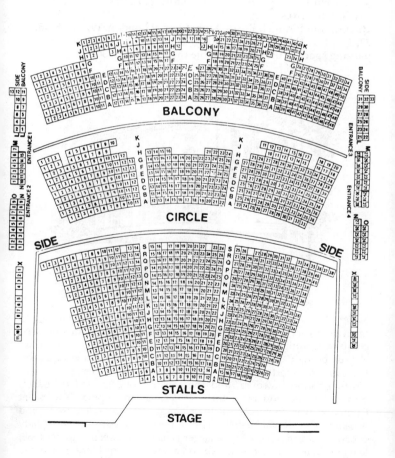

Sadler's Wells Theatre

Rosebery Avenue, EC1R 4TN

**Box Office: 10.30 to 19.30 hrs
Mon to Sat or until 6.30 pm
when no evening performance.
Tel: 278 8916
Credit Cards: Yes**

**Bars: 3
Catering: Snacks and Buffet
Restaurant
Seating: 1,500**

**Underground: Angel. Buses: From Central London: 19, 30, 38, 43,
73, 104, 171, 214, 277, 279. Parking: There is usually ample street
parking space in the vicinity of the theatre after 18.30.**

Sadler's Wells had a varied career, going from great peaks of glory to
great depths of depression and disrepute. From 1916, it deteriorated
completely until nine years later, the amazing Lilian Baylis – who had
already brought drama, opera and ballet to *The Old Vic* – decided to do
the same for North London. Drama proved to be less popular in
North London however, and the theatre concentrated on ballet,
under the direction of Ninette de Valois, and opera. The Ballet
Company was so successful that it moved to Covent Garden and
became The Royal Ballet. The Opera Company was equally
prosperous and moved to the larger *London Coliseum* in August 1968,
leaving *Sadler's Wells* free to take on a new responsibility, namely to

act as host to renowned Ballet, Mime and Opera companies from all over the world.

Sadler's Wells is the home of Sadler's Wells Royal Ballet which presents two seasons at the theatre each year; other companies appearing on a regular basis include London Contemporary Dance Theatre, Ballet Rambert and New Sadler's Wells Opera.

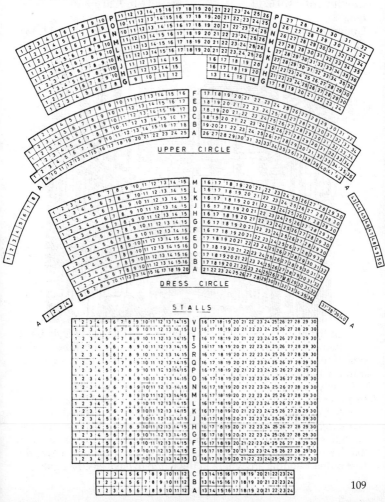

UPPER CIRCLE

DRESS CIRCLE

STALLS

Savoy Theatre

Savoy Court, Strand, WC2R 0ET

Box Office: 10.00 to 20.00 hrs
Tel: 836 8888
Credit Cards: 379 6219
Bars: 4

Catering: Theatre/Dinner
package – Simpsons in the
Strand 6 to 7.30 pm
Seating: 1,122

Underground: Covent Garden, Embankment. Buses: 1, 6, 9, 11, 13, 15, 77, 170, 176.

Two of the many remarkable achievements of Richard D'Oyly Carte are connected with *The Savoy Theatre* – the establishment of a permanent 'home' for Gilbert and Sullivan's comic operas and the introduction of electric light to theatres.

D'Oyly Carte, S.W. Gilbert and Arthur Sullivan, while working together at *The Royalty Theatre* had already formed The Comedy Opera Company. When the lease on *The Royalty* expired, D'Oyly Carte decided not to renew it but instead to build his own theatre. Architect C.J. Phipps was commissioned for the design, and when *The Savoy* – situated on the Thames Embankment – opened, it was the first public building anywhere in the world to have electric light.

AUDITORIUM PLAN

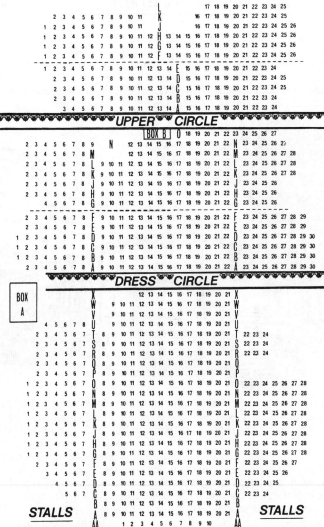

Shaftesbury Theatre

Shaftesbury Avenue, WC2H 8DP

Box Office: 10.00 to 20.00 hrs
Tel: 379 5399
Credit Cards: Yes

Bars: 5
Catering: Coffee
Seating: 1,391

Underground: Tottenham Court Road, Covent Garden. Buses: 8, 10, 14, 19, 22, 24, 25, 29, 38, 73, 134, 176.

The musical "Hair" could be said, quite literally, to have 'brought the house down' for, just as it was about to celebrate its 2,000th performance at *The Shaftesbury Theatre* in July 1973, part of the ceiling gave way and the theatre had to be closed! This event had rather serious implications for, only a few months previously, *The Shaftesbury* had been under threat of demolition when there were plans to redevelop the site. However, with massive public support and the efforts of the Save London's Theatres Campaign, it was judged to be a ". . . building of special architectural or historical interest . . ." The result was that the theatre was able to reopen in December 1974.

AUDITORIUM PLAN

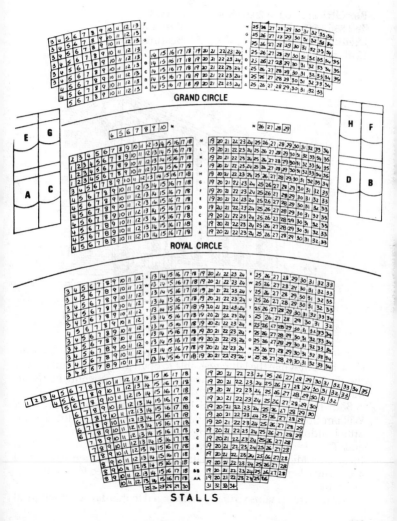

GRAND CIRCLE

ROYAL CIRCLE

STALLS

St Martin's Theatre

West Street, Cambridge Circus, WC2H 8DP

Box Office: 10.00 to 20.00 hrs
Tel: 836 1443
Credit Cards: Yes
Underground: Leicester Square.

Bars: 3
Catering: No
Seating: 550
Buses: 1, 14, 19, 22, 24, 29, 38.

The St. Martin's Theatre was planned to 'pair' with *The Ambassadors* close by, but while the latter was able to open in 1913, the outbreak of the First World War delayed the completion and opening of *The St. Martin's* until 23rd November, 1916.

Both theatres were designed by the sensitive hand of architect William Sprague, who was responsible for so many of the elegant little London theatres – including *The Albery*, *The Aldwych*, *The Strand* and *The Globe*. By now the great era of Victorian and Edwardian theatre-building was coming to its close – French influence had died away and a harder, more classical style known as 'neo-Georgian' was evolving.

The theatre remains virtually unchanged to this day, charming and cosy with its red seating and dark wood panelling. At present it houses the world's longest running play "The Mousetrap".

UPPER CIRCLE

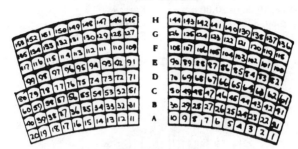

DRESS CIRCLE

STALLS

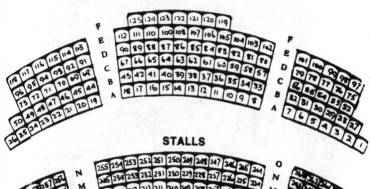

Strand Theatre

Aldwych, WC2B 5LD

Box Office: 10.00 to 20.00 hrs
Tel: 836 2660, 836 4143, 836 5190
Credit Cards: Yes

Bars: 4
Catering: Yes
Seating: 1,061

Underground: Covent Garden, Temple, Holborn. Buses: 1, 6, 9, 11, 13, 15, 77, 170, 176, 188, 239, 305.

On 22nd May, 1905 *The Strand* (although it was known as *The Waldorf* until 1909) became the first theatre to be built in the new Aldwych. It was designed by William Sprague as one of a pair – the other being *The Aldwych Theatre* – each occupying a similar corner site and separated by the Waldorf Hotel. During this period, a great deal of construction work was being carried out all over London and the Kingsway/Aldwych development was to be a distinctive feature of the Imperial capital.

Strand

The theatre has been redecorated a number of times – notably in 1930 – but overall has changed little since it was first built. Today, the auditorium is resplendent in turquoise, gold and cream with red seating. The Edwardian influence is also present in the foyer with its elegant statues and stairway, dominated by a large picture of London impresario, Henry Sherek.

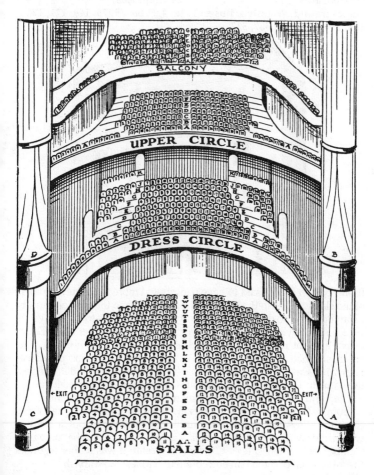

The Old Vic

Waterloo Road, SE1 8NB

Box Office: 10.00 to 20.00 hrs
Tel: 928 7616
Credit Cards: Yes
Underground: Waterloo. Buses: 1, 1a, 4, 5, 68, 70, 76, 149, 171, 176, 188, 239, 501, 502, 507, 513.

Bars: 3
Catering: Snacks Tel: 928 8197
Seating: 1,037

If one person can be said to have contributed more to the development of the classical British theatre in modern times, then that person must be Lilian Baylis, who devoted almost forty years of her life to *The Old Vic*. In 1912, Lilian Baylis officially took over the theatre from her aunt, Emma Cons, a social reformer and herself something of a pioneer. In 1880, when she had come to *The New Victoria Palace* (as it was previously known), it was a bawdy, disreputable house. She refurbished it, changed the name to *The Royal Victoria Hall and Coffee Tavern* and turned it into "... a cheap and decent place of amusement on strict temperance lines . . ."

From 1976 the theatre had various managements, including the touring company, Prospect Productions, until May 1981 when public subsidy was withdrawn altogether. *The Old Vic* was closed from that date until October 1983 when, after a £2.5 million facelift, it was reopened under the ownership of Canadian entrepreneur 'Honest' Ed Mirvish.

AUDITORIUM PLAN

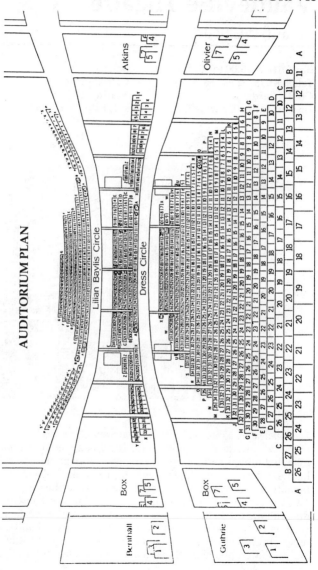

Vaudeville Theatre

Strand, WC2R 0NH

Box Office: 10.00 to 20.00 hrs
Tel: 836 9987 & 836 5645
Credit Cards: Yes

Bars: 3
Catering: No
Seating: 694

Underground: Charing Cross. Buses: 1, 6, 9, 11, 13, 15, 77, 170, 176.

The Vaudeville, along with other theatres built around 1870, signified in many ways the ending of an era. The theatre building boom which followed brought with it many changes – foreign design influences, higher safety standards and various technological improvements, notably the introduction of electric light. Nevertheless, at the time, The Vaudeville's own new system of lighting was something of an innovation. *The Vaudeville* was completely refurbished in 1969, and with its elegant gold and blue (seats) and glorious chandelier in the foyer – is undoubtedly one of London's most delightful little theatres, and is now owned by Michael Codron and David Sutton.

Vaudeville

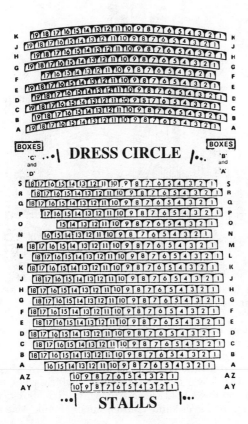

...| **UPPER CIRCLE** |...

BOXES ...| **DRESS CIRCLE** |... BOXES
'C'   'B'
and   and
'D'   'A'

...| **STALLS** |...

Victoria Palace Theatre

Victoria Street, SW1E 5EA

Box Office: 10.00 to 20.00 hrs   **Bars: 5**
Tel: 834 1317   **Catering: Snacks**
Credit Cards: Yes   **Seating: 1,565**
Underground: Victoria. Buses: 2, 10, 11, 16, 24, 25, 29, 36, 38, 39, 52,
149, 181, 185, 500,
503, 506, 507, 509.

The period 1880 until 1910 saw the music halls reach their peak in Britain. Hundreds of these lively establishments were built all over the country – to a far greater extent than were theatres or opera houses. Music halls were derived largely from the taverns, where food and drink automatically accompanied entertainment, and it was from just such origins *The Victoria Palace* evolved.

In 1910, Alfred Butt bought The Royal Standard Music Hall – previously The Royal Standard Tavern – which were the oldest premises in London to hold a licence for a music hall. Butt demolished the building, however, and commissioned Frank Matcham, the architect of numerous music halls all over the country, to design *The Victoria Palace*.

The classical facade once included a statue of the famous ballerina Pavlova, who made her first London appearance at the theatre – but she was superstitious and refused to look up at it when she passed by! (It was taken down in the blitz and subsequently lost.) *"The Era"* of 4th November, 1911 described the interior as combining "... a maximum of comfort and convenience with a prevailing note of simplicity ... The entrance hall through which the visitor passes to the stalls, dress circle and boxes has walls of grey marble with embellishments of gold mosaic and pillars of white Sicilian marble ..."

Today, *The Victoria Palace* is a rich and atmospheric theatre, retaining much of its original style – the auditorium heavy and opulent and the foyer bright and elegant.

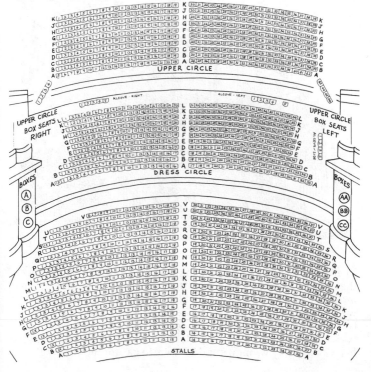

Westminster Theatre

Palace Street, Buckingham Palace Road, SW1 5JB

Box Office: 10.00 to 20.00 hrs
Tel: 834 0283
Credit Cards: 834 0048

Bars: 1
Catering: Snacks and Restaurant:
Lunch 12.00 to 14.00 hrs; Dinner
before performance 18.00 hrs.
(reservations necessary)
Seating: 585

Underground: Victoria. Buses: 2, 10, 11, 16, 24, 25, 29, 36, 38, 39, 52, 149, 181, 185, 500, 503, 506, 507, 509.

In the early twenties the cinema age had dawned. A number of theatres had already been converted and many more new cinemas, including The St. James's Picture House, later *The Westminster Theatre,* were being built. The St. James's, which opened in 1923 was constructed on the site of an old chapel – the origins of which dated back to 1776 when the extrovert Reverend Dodd used the proceeds of his wife's lottery winnings and a legacy to pay for the building!

Eventually, after being a chapel-of-ease for St. Peter's, Eaton Square, it was sold in 1921.

In 1931, the building was taken over by Anmer Hall who transformed it into a theatre, adapting the crypt into dressing rooms and a green room and incorporating a circle into the auditorium. Today, *The Westminster* which Hall named after his old public school, is a delightful little theatre with its chandelier and tasteful auditorium decor of terra-cotta, pink and red. Redecorated and refurbished 1986. There is a spacious restaurant and coffee/tea shop, open to theatregoers and non-patrons alike – and modern audio-visual facilities make the theatre a popular venue for business conventions and Induction Loop for Deaf patrons is now installed. Easy access for wheelchair patrons.

AUDITORIUM PLAN

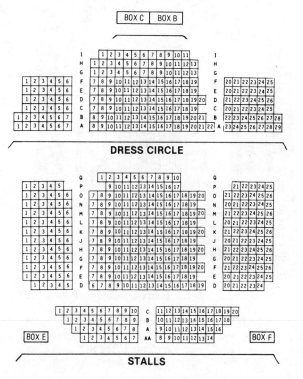

125

Whitehall Theatre

Whitehall, SW1A 2DY

Box Office: 10.00 to 20.00 hrs   **Bars: 2**
Tel: 867 1119   **Catering: No**
Credit Cards: Yes   **Seating: 608**
Underground: Charing Cross. Buses: 3, 11, 12, 24, 29, 39, 53, 77, 77A, 88, 159, 170, 172.

Opened in 1930, the theatre was built on the original site of "Ye Old Ship Tavern".

Television and theatre audiences of the fifties and sixties will be especially familiar with the *Whitehall Theatre* – home of so many of Brian Rix's popular "Whitehall Farces", including "The Reluctant Heroes", "One For The Pot", "Dry Rot", "Chase Me Comrade" and "Simple Spyman".

Whitehall

These farces continued to be staged until the end of the 1960's when impresario Paul Raymond took over management and started with nude productions for some years. In 1983 with the Falklands war, the theatre became a war museum. In 1985 again new management took over who extensively refurbished the theatre, returning it to its original Art Deco grandeur. It is a firm favourite with theatregoers and remains a theatre renowned for farce.

AUDITORIUM PLAN

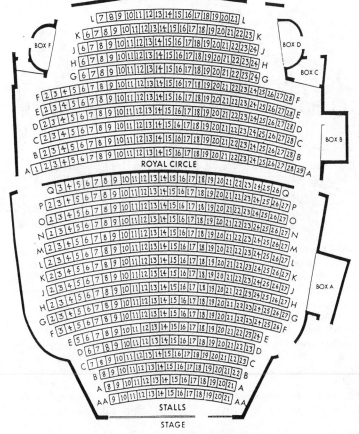

Wyndham's Theatre

Charing Cross Road, WC2H 0DA

Box Office: 10.00 to 20.00 hrs
Tel: 867 1116
Credit Cards: 867 1111
Underground: Leicester Square. Buses: 1, 14, 19, 22, 24, 29, 38, 176.

Bars: 2
Catering: No
Seating: 759

When the Marquess of Salisbury was asked if he would permit a theatre to be built on his land between St. Martin's Lane and Charing Cross Road, he was not particularly enthusiastic – unless it be for Charles Wyndham, the actor manager, whose dramatic talents he greatly admired.

In fact, Wyndham, manager of *The Criterion Theatre* for some years, already had plans to build his own theatre, so the choice of site was an obvious one. The architect Sprague was commissioned to design the theatre on the same plot of land where he was later to be responsible for *The New Theatre* (now *The Albery*). Sprague's work was usually a blend of styles, but at the turn of the century he was particularly influenced by the wave of French fashion – and this is reflected in his theatre. *"The Era"* of 18th November, 1899 says ". . . The scheme of decoration is that of

Louis XVI . . . The ceiling of the auditorium contains paintings after Boucher, which are illuminated by a ring of concealed electric lights and a central sunlight covered by a crystal pendant . . ." Today, *Wyndham's* is one of the loveliest of London's small, intimate theatres.

AUDITORIUM PLAN

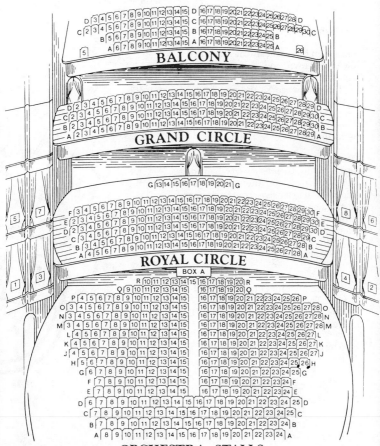

BALCONY

GRAND CIRCLE

ROYAL CIRCLE

BOX A

ORCHESTRA STALLS

LONDON FRINGE

'Fringe' or 'alternative theatre' are terms widely used to describe entertainment and performances that are not part of the traditional West End Theatre Network. The movements began in the late 60's in small studios and converted experimental venues as a reaction to and to complement the standard fare offered by the well known theatre establishment.

Since then fringe theatre has assumed a life of its own and London offers a wealth of talent committed to presenting innovative works and new ways of looking at old favourites. Often working within tight budgets and emphasis is on the quality and intimacy of performance.

Details about fringe shows are to be found in the *Guardian* every Saturday on the Arts page, the Alternative Theatre column, but extensive coverage is given in magazines such as *"Time Out"* and *"City Limits"*. This information includes telephone numbers, how to get there and a short synopsis of what to expect from the show.

The *British Alternative Theatre Directory* (published by John Offord Publications Ltd., 12 The Avenue, Eastbourne BN21 3YA) is a comprehensive guide to all the fringe has to offer.

Map by courtesy of *Theatre Despatch*, 853 0750.

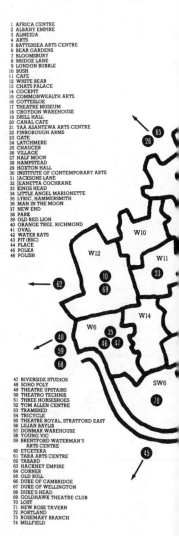

1 AFRICA CENTRE
2 ALBANY EMPIRE
3 ALMEIDA
4 ARTS
5 BATTERSEA ARTS CENTRE
6 BEAR GARDENS
7 BLOOMSBURY
8 BRIDGE LANE
9 LONDON BUBBLE
10 BUSH
11 CAFE
12 WHITE BEAR
13 CHATS PALACE
14 COCKPIT
15 COMMONWEALTH ARTS
16 COTTESLOE
17 THEATRE MUSEUM
18 CROYDON WAREHOUSE
19 DRILL HALL
20 CANAL CAFE
21 YAA ASANTEWA ARTS CENTRE
22 FINBOROUGH ARMS
23 GATE
24 LATCHMERE
25 CHAUCER
26 VILLAGE
27 HALF MOON
28 HAMPSTEAD
29 HOXTON HALL
30 INSTITUTE OF CONTEMPORARY ARTS
31 JACKSONS LANE
32 JEANETTA COCHRANE
33 KINGS HEAD
34 LITTLE ANGEL MARIONETTE
35 LYRIC, HAMMERSMITH
36 MAN IN THE MOON
37 NEW END
38 PARK
39 OLD RED LION
40 ORANGE TREE, RICHMOND
41 OVAL
42 WATER RATS
43 PIT (RSC)
44 PLACE
45 POLKA
46 POLISH

47 RIVERSIDE STUDIOS
48 SOHO POLY
49 THEATRE UPSTAIRS
50 THEATRO TECHNIS
51 THREE HORSESHOES
52 TOM ALLEN CENTRE
53 TRAMSHED
54 TRICYCLE
55 THEATRE ROYAL, STRATFORD EAST
56 LILIAN BAYLIS
57 DONMAR WAREHOUSE
58 YOUNG VIC
59 BRENTFORD WATERMAN'S ARTS CENTRE
60 ETCETERA
61 TARA ARTS CENTRE
62 TABARD
63 HACKNEY EMPIRE
64 CORNER
65 OLD BULL
66 DUKE OF CAMBRIDGE
67 DUKE OF WELLINGTON
68 DUKE'S HEAD
69 GOLDHAWK THEATRE CLUB
70 LOST
71 NEW ROSE TAVERN
72 PORTLAND
73 ROSEMARY BRANCH
74 MILLFIELD

THEATRE DESPATCH
P.O. BOX 633
LONDON SE7 7HE
081-853 0750

THEATRES

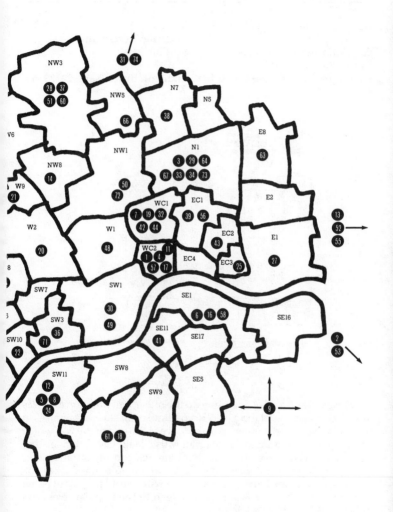

Players' Theatre

The Arches, Villiers Street, WC2N 6NG

Box Office: 10.00 to 20.00 hrs
Tel: 839 1134
Credit Cards: Visa/Access
Closed Mondays only.

Bars: 2
Catering: Restaurant
Seating: 260

Underground: Charing Cross, Embankment. Buses: 3, 12, 24, 29, 53, 88, 159.

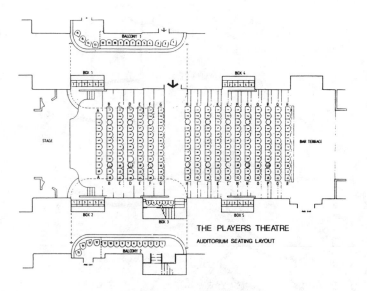

THE PLAYERS THEATRE
AUDITORIUM SEATING LAYOUT

The Players' Theatre Club is a tribute to the music hall tradition and was founded in its present form in 1936 and housed in several premises in the West End before taking up a residence at the end of the war which had once housed a famous Victorian Music Hall, Gatti's Under-the-Arches. In addition to Victorian Pantomimes and Melodrama's *The Players'* has produced many musicals. It has re-opened after the redevelopment of Charing Cross station with the adage "Slap! Bang! Here we are again!" It was regularly seen in the popular television programme "The Good Old Days".

Other Entertainment Venues

Wembley Stadium and Wembley Arena Complex
North Circular Road, Wembley, Middx.

Box Office: 9.30 to 21.00 hrs	Bars: Several
Tel: 081 900 1234	Catering: Snacks
Credit Cards: Yes	Grandstand Restaurant/
Tickets also from Wembley	Wembley Arena Rest.
Ticket Shop, Virgin Megastore	Fast Food Carvery.
in Oxford St. (071 862 0202)	

The Stadium: Arena, Conference Centre, Exhibition Hall, you have it all here at Wembley! Cup Finals, Music Festivals, Concerts, Competitions, Exhibitions – for constantly updated information service call 0898-600500.

Underground: Wembley Park by Metropolitan line or Wembley Central by Bakerloo line. BR: Wembley Central from Euston or Liverpool St., or Wembley Stadium from Marylebone.

The Wembley Stadium Complex is situated on the North Circular Road with easy access to the M40, M4, M1, A1 and M25 Motorways.

Buses: Good choice of buses.

Parking: For over 5,000 vehicles at Wembley Stadium Complex. Cars parked in local streets on major event days may be towed away.

Hammersmith Odeon
Queen Caroline Street, W6 9QH

Box Office: 11.00 to 20.00 hrs	Bars: One
Tel: 081 748 4081	Catering: Snacks
Credit Cards: 081 741 4868	Seating: 3,485

Underground: Hammersmith (Piccadilly, District, Metropolitan)

Buses: Good choice. NCP available.

Hammersmith Odeon is a major Concert Venue; Jazz, Orchestral, Rock etc.

London Arena
Limeharbour, London E14 9TH

Box Office: 10.00 to 20.00 hrs	Bars: Six
Tel: 071 538 1212	Catering: Snacks
Credit Cards: Yes	Seating: Flexible – up to 11,000

Underground: Tower Hill or Stratford on to Docklands Light Railway to Crossharbour station. (Dockland Railway closes 9.30pm and buses provided to Mile End Underground Station)

London Arena is a new Multipurpose indoor venue located in Docklands development zone for every type of entertainment, concerts, sporting events, exhibitions etc.

Barbican Hall

Silk Street, London EC2Y 8DS

Advance Booking: 638 8891   **For general information see
'Barbican Centre' – page 34**

The Barbican Hall is home to the London Symphony Orchestra, who
perform over 100 concerts throughout the year.
  The auditorium, seating 2026 in three curved, raked tiers, provides

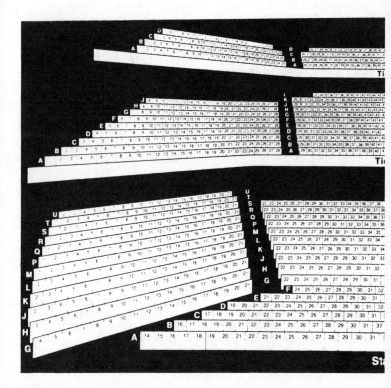

Barbican Hall

excellent sightlines combined with a degree of intimacy not usually to be found in a hall of this size. The interior decor of light-coloured pine contrasts attractively with the various dark tones of the extremely comfortable seating.

As well as the LSO season, the hall functions as a concert hall for a wide range of performances from solo recitals to symphony orchestras, and includes a range of light entertainment – especially jazz. The Barbican Hall also functions as a conference venue, and is equipped with simultaneous interpretation, amplification, broadcast and satellite relay, and projection facilities to meet the sophisticated requirements of today's conference organiser.

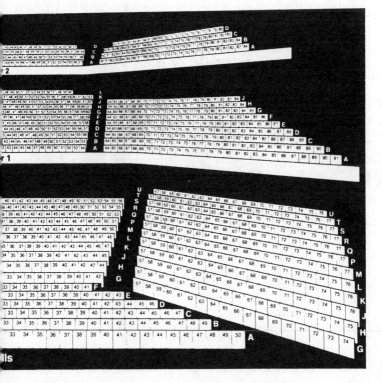

Royal Albert Hall

Kensington Gore, SW7 2AP

Map 5

Booking Office:
9.00 to 21.00 hrs.
Tel: 589 8212
Enquiries: 589 3203
£1 charge per booking
Credit Cards: 589 9465

Bars: 10
Catering: Snacks
Seating: 5,000 approx.

Underground: Kensington High Street, Knightsbridge, South Kensington. Buses: Direct 9, 10, 52. To Palace Gate 49; To Kensington Church Street 27, 28, 31; To South Kensington 14, 30, 45, 74.

A half hour guided tour is available throughout the day – visit to the Queen's Box, the Royal Retiring Room, special displays and ends with a complimentary drink in the Prince Consort Restaurant. Prices: £2.50 Adults (inc. Senior Citizens), £1.50 Students/Children. (Times 9.30 - 5.00. 26th May - 5th October)

A one hour tour is available to groups of 20+ which must be booked in advance through the Tour Office. This is a more detailed tour and includes a special exhibition of Royal photographs. Prices: £3.75 Adults (inc. Senior Citizens), £2.00 Students/Children. This Tour does not include complimentary drink.

The Prince Consort Restaurant is open for visitors from 9.30am every day serving morning coffee, lunches and afternoon teas.

Royal Albert Hall

It had been the wish of Prince Albert, Queen Victoria's beloved husband, to provide the nation with an Arts and Science Centre. Although he died before his dream became reality the inscription high up on the outside of *The Royal Albert Hall* remembers ". . . This hall was erected for the advancement of the Arts and Sciences and works of industry of all nations in fulfilment of the intention of Albert, Prince Consort . . ."

With the £180,000 profit resulting from the Great International Exhibition of 1851 (itself initiated by Prince Albert), an estate was purchased in South Kensington and various plans drawn up for the proposed Arts and Science Centre under the guidance of Prince Albert. On his death in 1861, work came to a halt but the scheme was again taken up by his son, the Prince of Wales in 1865, and construction duly started in 1867. The red brick and terra-cotta building, which took four years to complete, is in the Italian Renaissance style, and some believe it is based on the Colosseum in Rome.

Queen Victoria opened *The Royal Albert Hall* on 29th March, 1871 in the presence of the entire Royal Family and the Prime Minister, Mr Gladstone. Since then, it has had five reigning monarchs as its patron – and remains a monument to the Victorian Age which is completly unlike any other. It is awe-inspiring and it is magnificent. Step inside and one is immediately overwhelmed by the strong sense of patriotism and tradition which dominate its still intensely Victorian atmosphere.

The Royal Albert Hall has been used for religious and political events, athletic contests, banquets, exhibitions and, most of all, for music. For over a century, many of the world's greatest celebrities have appeared here.

In July 1871, the first recital was played on the Great Organ – described at the time as being ". . . the greatest and most complete instrument in the world . . ." In 1877 came the unforgettable Wagner concerts, conducted by the composer himself, with vocalists from the Beyreuth Festival. In 1886, there was the long series of Patti concerts which continued until her retirement. Since 1941, (following the bombing of the previous venue, *The Queen's Hall*), there has been the annual season of Henry Wood Promenade Concerts, Festivals, Sporting Occasions, Popular Concerts etc.

Royal Albert Hall

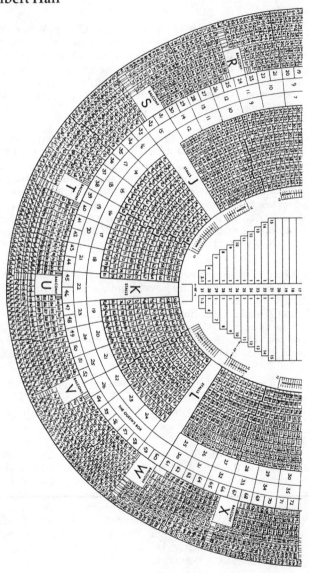

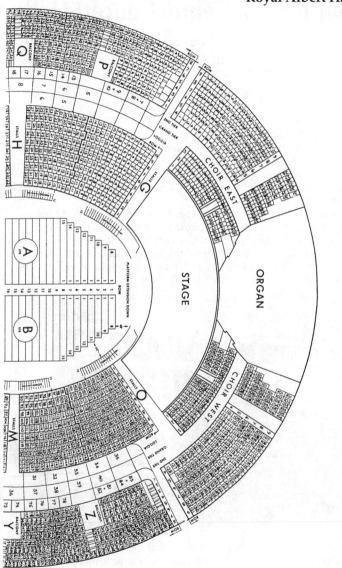

South Bank Centre Concert Halls

Royal Festival Hall, Queen Elizabeth Hall and Purcell Room – South Bank, SE1 8XX

Box Office: 10.00 to 21.00 hrs
7 days a week.
Tel: 928 8800

Information: 928 3002
Credit Cards: Yes

Food and Drink: Review Restaurant: 12.00am-12.00pm. Riverside Cafe: 10.00am-8.00pm. Coffee Lounge: 10.00am-10.00pm. Festival Buffet, Salt Beef and Pasta Bars: 12.00am-2.30pm, 5.30pm-10.00pm. Licensed bars open normal hours. Foyers Open: From 10.00am – free lunchtime music daily 12.00-2.00pm. Commuter Jazz 5.15pm-6.45pm Fridays. Exhibitions and shops.

Underground: Waterloo (Northern, Bakerloo and BR Waterloo & City Line) and Embankment (Northern, Bakerloo, District and Circle). British Rail: Waterloo. Car Parking: ECP car parks in Jubilee Gardens, beside Hungerford Bridge and under Hayward Gallery (all off Belvedere Road). Computer Cab: Booking service at RFH. Mailing List: £6.00 pa (921 0655/6)

It is hard to imagine that, just after the war, the site which now houses London's handsome South Bank complex was little more than an area of dereliction. The concept of The South Bank Centre Concert Halls was originally conceived in 1948 under Mr Attlee's Government, when the London County Council offered to provide a permanent concert hall as their contribution to the Festival of Britain, planned for 1951. The Royal Festival Hall, opened in 1951, now forms part of the South Bank Centre which incorporates the three Concert Halls, the Voice Box and Poetry Library, the Hayward Gallery, the National Theatre, the National Film Theatre and the Museum of the Moving Image. The South Bank Centre is the world's largest centre for the arts. The Concert Halls, Voice Box and Hayward Gallery are administered by the South Bank Board, a constituent part of the Arts Council of Great Britain.

Royal Festival Hall/Auditorium

Clement Attlee laid the foundation stone of the Royal Festival Hall in 1949, and two years later the ceremonial opening took place at an inaugural concert attended by King George VI and H.M. Queen Elizabeth. The Archbishop of Canterbury conducted a Service of Dedication and this was followed by a programme of British music.

Designed by Sir Robert Matthew and Dr Leslie Martin, the Royal Festival Hall has a large auditorium and can accommodate 2,909 people during the concert season. The hall is resplendent in elm panelling and red leather and boasts excellent acoustics which in 1964 were given the added advantage of an 'assisted resonance system'. The proscenium arch can be erected for ballet or other stage productions. Approximately 500 performances are given annually, of which about two-thirds are symphony concerts. The Festival Hall Organ, designed by Ralph Downes was installed in 1954 and inaugurated on 24th March of that year.

Royal Festival Hall (Auditorium)

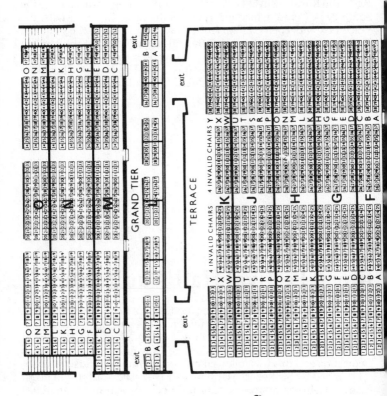

Red Side

Green Side

Royal Festival Hall

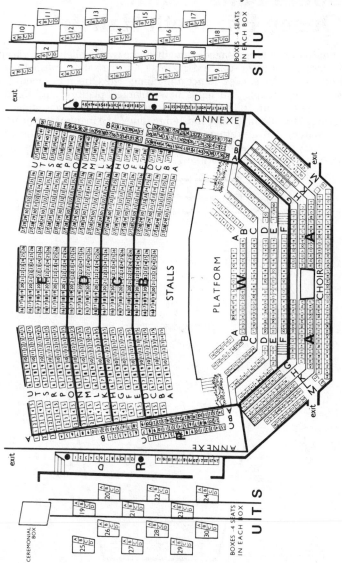

South Bank Centre/ Queen Elizabeth Hall

Some 800 events are staged annually in the two smaller auditoria and include small orchestral and chamber music recitals, music theatre and film performances, dance and mime. The Queen Elizabeth Hall seats 1,054 people and has a new enlarged platform and lighting facilities enabling full scale productions of opera. It also has projection facilities for 70mm, 35mm and 16mm films. The inaugural concert on 1st March, 1967 was attended by Queen Elizabeth II and the opening concert included a programme of works by such composers as Purcell, Bliss, Arne and Britten.

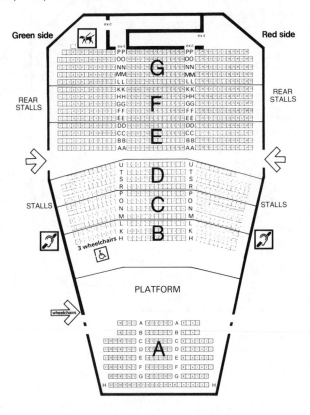

South Bank Centre/ Purcell Room

The Purcell Room, with a seating capacity of 372 is a small intimate hall, used for recitals by solo artistes and chamber groups. It is also a popular venue for talks, lectures and cabaret.

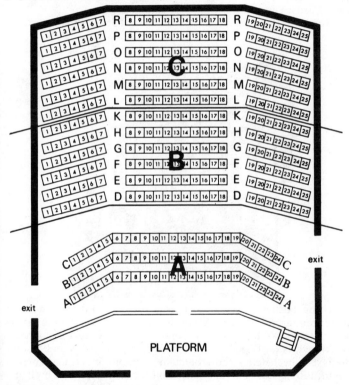

The Voice Box

In November 1988 the Arts Council Poetry Library found a new home on Level 5 of the Royal Festival Hall and the Voice Box opened providing a new venue for literature events. There are 77 seats and approximately 120 events per year.

Wigmore Hall

Wigmore Street, W1H 9DF

Map 1

Box Office: 10.00 to 20.30 hrs
Tel: 935 2141
Credit Cards: Yes
Underground: Bond Street. Buses: All Oxford Street Buses.

Bars: 1
Catering: Snacks and Coffee
Seating: 540

The name Bechstein brings to most people's minds an image of magnificent grand pianos – but probably rather fewer people realise that Frederick Wilhelm Carl Bechstein was also the creator of what is now known as *The Wigmore Hall*. *The Bechstein Hall* opened in 1901 on a site next to Bechstein's showrooms in Wigmore Street. Designed in beautiful Renaissance style by Mr. Collcutt F.R.I.B.A. and built at a cost of almost £100,000 its near-perfect acoustics soon made it one of London's most popular venues for solo recitals and chamber music. Today's *Wigmore Hall*, still retaining its abundance of marble and alabaster, is as glorious as ever. When empty, one is struck by its innate elegance and dignity, yet when the hall is crowded with enthusiastic concert-goers, the atmosphere changes to one of great intimacy.

Wigmore Hall

The platform of *The Wigmore Hall* has welcomed most of this century's greatest performers including, since the twenties, a guitar recital by Segovia, numerous performances by Artur Rubinstein (who made his début here in 1912 when aged 25), and a never to be forgotten appearance of Prokofiev in 1931. Elisabeth Schwarzkopf made her London début at *The Wigmore Hall* in 1948, as did Daniel Barenboim in 1958 (aged 15 and wearing short trousers!) From the fifties works by Benjamin Britten were heard, sung by Peter Pears to the composer's accompaniment. *The Wigmore Hall's* 75th Anniversary celebrations in 1976 included special recitals by Artur Rubinstein, Elisabeth Schwarztkopf, Julian Bream and Peter Pears.

AUDITORIUM PLAN

PLAN OF GROUND FLOOR

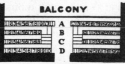

PLAN OF BALCONY

Bus and Tube Night Services

THEATRELAND

Theatreland is easily accessible by Bus or Tube. Information and free maps and leaflets can also be obtained from London Transport's chain of **Travel Information Centres** at many central London stations, at Heathrow Airport and at West Croydon Bus Station. A new centre is open at Liverpool Street Underground. Avoid traffic jams and parking problems and take a Bus or Tube to a West End show. Afterwards why not grab a bite to eat and enjoy a drink before you catch the last bus or tube.

Where to Eat

Where to eat when going to the theatre, need not be a problem!

Whether you are looking for 'fast-food', 'pub-grub' or say, French cuisine, the following pages list them in alphabetical order with Map for pin-pointing each venue near the relevant theatre.

Theatres have a star symbol and restaurants a black dot

Pub hours: 11.00 - 15.00, 17.30-23.00 (since de-regulation, can vary)
Sun: 12.00-14.00, 1900-22.30

Restaurant hours: 17.00-23.30
This is usually last-order time and not closing time

Pre-theatre set meals are available at some restaurants at very reasonable prices so check when making reservations.

Symbols: £ = £10.00 and under, ££ = £20.00, £££ = about £25.00, £££* = over £25.00 (wine is not included).

Credit Cards: A - Access, AX - American Express, B - Barclay (Visa and others), DC - Diner's Card.

Note: Add prefix 071 when dialling outside the London Area.

Where to Eat

AU JARDIN DES GOURMETS
French ££*　　　　　　**Map 1-50**
Closed Sat L. Sun (must book)
Credit Cards: A, AX, B, DC.
5 Greek St.　　　　　　**Tel: 437 1816**

BEOTY'S
Greek £££　　　　　　**Map 4-52**
12.15-15.00, 17.30-23.30
Closed Sun
Credit Cards: A, AX, B, DC.
79 St. Martin's Lane　　**Tel: 836 8768**

BRAGANZA
International (Restaurant) ££　**Map 1-54**
(Brasserie) ££
12.30-14.30, 18.15-23.15
Closed Sunday
Credit Cards: A, AX, B, DC.
56 Frith St.　　　　　　**Tel: 437 5412**

CAFE FISH
Restaurant ££　　　　　**Map 3-85**
Wine Bar Piano Bar
11.30-15.00, 18.00-23.30
Wine Bar 11.30-15.00, 17.30-23.00
Credit Cards: A, AX, B, DC.
39 Patton St.　　　　　**Tel: 930 3999**

CAFE ROYAL GRILL
Grills £££*　　　　　　**Map 3-55**
12.00-15.00, 18.00-23.00
Closed No (must book)
Credit Cards: A, AX, B, DC.
68 Regent St.　　　　　**Tel: 439 6320**

CHEZ SOLANGE
French £££　　　　　　**Map 4-56**
12.15-15.15, 17.30-00.15
Closed Sun (must book)
Credit Cards: A, AX, B, DC.
35 Cranbourne St.　　　**Tel: 836 0542**

CHUEN-CHENG-KU
Chinese ££　　　　　　**Map 3-57**
11.00-23.30
Closed No
Credit Cards: Yes
17 Wardour St.　　　　**Tel: 437 1398**

THEATRES:		
	8-2	*Cambridge*
2-4	*Albery*	9-4	*Coliseum*
4-2	*Ambassador*	10-3	*Comedy*
5-3	*Apollo*	11-3	*Criterion*
6-4	*Arts*	33-2	*Donmar*
7-1	*Astoria*	15-4	*Duke of York's*

Where to Eat – Piccadilly · Soho · St. Martin's Lane

CORK & BOTTLE (Wine Bar)
Buffet £   **Map 4-58**
11.00-14.45, 17.30-22.45
Open Sun: 12.00-14.30, 17.00-22.30
Credit Cards: A, AX, B, DC.
44 Cranbourne St.   **Tel: 734 7807**

DU ROLLO
French £   **Map 1-60**
12.30-15.00, 17.45-23.15
Closed Sun (must book)
Credit Cards: A, AX, B, DC.
20 Greek St.   **Tel: 734 6991**

ESTORIL da Luigi & Roberto
Italian ££   **Map 3-63**
12.00-2.30. Sat 18.00-23.00
Credit Cards: A, AX, B, DC.
3 Denman St.   **Tel: 437 8700**

GAY HUSSAR
Hungarian   **Map 1-62**
12.30-14.30, 17.30-23.30
Closed Sun
Credit Cards: No
2 Greek St.   **Tel: 437 0973**

IVY
French £££*   **Map 2-64**
12.15-14.30, 18.15-23.15
Closed Sat L. Sun (must book)
Credit Cards: A, AX, B, DC.
1-5 West St.   **Tel: 836 4751**

KETTNERS
Haute Cuisine (Popular)   **Map 2-65**
££
11.00-24.00
Closed No
Credit Cards: A, AX, B, DC.
29 Romilly St.   **Tel: 734 6112**

LA CAPANNINA
Italian ££   **Map 1-67**
12.00-15.00, 18.00-23.30
Closed Sat L. Sun (must book)
Credit Cards: A, AX, B, DC.
24 Romilly St.   **Tel: 437 2473**

Where to Eat – Piccadilly · Soho · St. Martin's Lane

L'EPICURE
French (Flambe's) ££   **Map 1-68**
12.00-14.30, 18.00-23.15
Closed Sat L. Sun (must book)
Credit Cards: A, AX, B, DC.
28 Frith St.   **Tel: 437 2829**

L'ESCARGOT
French £££   **Map 1-69**
12.15-14.30, 18.30-23.15
Closed Sat L. Sun (must book)
Credit Cards: A, AX, B, DC.
48 Greek St.   **Tel: 437 2679**

MANZI
Seafood ££   **Map 3-70**
12.00-14.40, 17.30-23.30
Closed Sun L. (must book)
Credit Cards: A, AX, B, DC.
1 Leicester St.   **Tel: 734 0224/5/6**

PELICAN
French ££   **Map 4-66**
11.00-24.15
Open 7 days a week
Credit Cards: A, AX, B, DC.
45 St. Martin's Lane   **Tel: 379 0309**

POON'S & CO.
Chinese ££   **Map 3-76**
12.00-23.30
Closed Sun
Credit Cards: No
4 Leicester St.   **Tel: 437 1528**

RUGANTINO
Italian £££   **Map 1-78**
12.00-14.30, 18.30-23.30
Closed Sun
Credit Cards: A, AX, B, DC.
26 Romilly St.   **Tel: 437 5302**

SHUTTLEWORTH'S at The Phoenix
English ££   **Map 2-61**
17.30-23.00. Sat 17.30-11.30
Credit Cards: A, AX, B, DC.
1 Phoenix St.   **Tel: 836 1077**

THEATRES:		8-2	*Cambridge*
2-4	*Albery*	9-4	*Coliseum*
4-2	*Ambassador*	10-3	*Comedy*
5-3	*Apollo*	11-3	*Criterion*
6-4	*Arts*	33-2	*Donmar*
7-1	*Astoria*	15-4	*Duke of York's*

The FARMHOUSE TABLE (Upstairs)
International/English £   Map 2-71
12.30-15.00, 17.30-23.30
Mon/Thurs
12.30-15.00, 17.30-24.00
Fri/Sat
190 Shaftesbury Ave   **Tel: 836 2652**

KANTARA TAVERNA (Downstairs)
Greek £   Map 2-71
same hours as Upstairs
Credit Cards: A, AX, B, DC.
190 Shaftesbury Ave   **Tel: 836 1149**

SOHO SOHO
French Restaurant -   Map 1-59
Cafe - Wine Bar
Rest: 12.00-23.30 Sat. Sat Dinner
Credit Cards: A, AX, B, DC.
11-13 Frith St.   **Tel: 494 3491**

SOLANGE
French ££ Brasserie -   Map 4-69
Wine Bar
12.00-23.45
Credit Cards: A, AX, B, DC.
11 St. Martin's Court   **Tel: 240 9936**

SWISS CENTRE (4 Restaurants)
Swiss, Gr.Fr. ££   Map 3-81
12.00-24.00
Closed No
Credit Cards: A, AX, B, DC.
Leicester Square   **Tel: 734 1291**

WHEELER'S
Seafood ££4   Map 1-84
12.30-14.30, 18.00-22.45
Closed No
Credit Cards: A, AX, B, DC.
19 Old Compton St.   **Tel: 437 2706**

WILTON'S
English £££   Map 3-49
12.30-14.15, 18.30-22.15
Credit Cards: A, AX, B, DC.
55 Jermyn St.   **Tel: 629 9955**

Where to Eat – Strand · Covent Garden

AJIMURA
Japanese ££   Map 5-89
12.00-14.30, 18.00-23.00
Closed Sat L. Sun (must book)
Credit Cards: A, AX, B, DC.
51-53 Shelton St.   **Tel: 240 0178**

BERTORELLI'S
Italian ££   Map 5-91
12.00-15.00, 17.45-23.30
Closed Sun (must book)
Credit Cards: A, AX, B, DC.
44 Floral St.   **Tel: 836 3969**

BERTORELLI'S (Wine Bar)
Buffet £   Map 5-91
Pub hours
Closed No
Credit Cards:
44 Floral St.   **Tel: 836 1868**

BOULESTIN
French £££*   Map 7-93
12.30-14.30, 19.30-23.15
Closed Sat L. Sun (must book)
Credit Cards: A, AX, B, DC.
1A Henrietta St.   **Tel: 836 7061**

BOSWELL'S
Coffee House   Map 7-92
8.00-23.00. Sat 9.30-6.30
8 Russell St.   **Tel: 240 0064**

BRAHMS & LIST (Wine Bar)
Buffet £   Map 5-94
11.30-15.00, 17.30-23.45
Closed Sat and L. Sun
Credit Cards: AX, B, A, DC.
19 Russell St.   **Tel: 240 3661**

FLOUNDERS
Seafood ££   Map 7-96
12.30-14.30, 17.00-1.00
Closed Sun (must book)
Credit Cards: A, AX, B, DC.
19 Tavistock St.   **Tel: 836 3925**

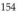

THEATRES:		
1-7	Adelphi	20-5 New London
3-6	Aldwych	26-6 Royalty
12-5	Drury Lane	27-5 Royal Opera
14-7	Duchess	29-7 Savoy
16-6	Fortune	31-8 Strand
		32-7 Vaudeville

FOOD FOR THOUGHT
Vegetarian £   **Map 5-88**
12.00-20.00
Closed Sat, Sun
Credit Cards: No
31 Neal St.   **Tel: 836 0239**

FRERE JACQUES
Seafood £££   **Map 7-97**
12.00-15.00, 18.00-23.30
Closed Sunday 14.30
Credit Cards: All Cards
38 Long Acre, C. Gdn   **Tel: 836 7823**

FRIDAY'S
The American Bistro £/££   **Map 7-90**
12.00-23.00, 7 days a week
Credit Cards: A, AX, B.
6 Bedford St.   **Tel: 379 0585**

GIARDINO'S
Italian £££   **Map 7-110**
12.00-23.30
Closed No
Credit Cards: All Cards
32 Long Acre, C. Gdn   **Tel: 836 8529**

JOE ALLENS
American ££   **Map 7-98**
12.00-01.00
Sunday 12.00-24.00 Closed Christmas
Credit Cards: No
13 Exeter St.   **Tel: 836 0651**

LE CAFE DES AMIS DU VIN
French ££   **Map 5-99**
11.30-23.30
Open Sun.
Credit Cards: A, AX, B, DC.
11 Hanover Pl.   **Tel: 379 3444**

LE CAFE DU JARDIN
French £££   **Map 7-100**
12.00-14.30, 17.30-23.30
Closed Sun and Sat Lunch
Credit Cards: A, AX, B, DC.
28 Wellington St.   **Tel: 836 8760**

Where to Eat – Strand · Covent Garden

L'OPERA
French £££   Map 5-102
12.15-14.30, 18.00-24.00
Closed Sat L. Sun (must book)
Credit Cards: A, AX, B, DC.
32 Queen St.   **Tel: 405 9020**

LUIGI'S
Italian £££   Map 7-103
12.00-15.00, 17.30-23.30
Closed Sun (must book)
Credit Cards: A, B.
15 Tavistock St.   **Tel: 240 1795**

MAGNO'S BRASSERIE
French ££   Map 5-104
12.00-14.30, 18.00-23.30
Closed Sat L. Sun
Credit Cards: A, AX, B, DC.
65a Long Acre   **Tel: 836 6077**

MAXWELLS
American £   Map 5-106
12.00-24.00
Closed No
Credit Cards: A, B.
16/17 Russell St.   **Tel: 836 0303**

MARQUIS OF ANGLESEY (Pub)
Buffet £   Map 5-105
Pub Hours
Closed No
Credit Cards: No
39 Bow St.   **Tel: 240 3216**

NAGS HEAD
No food evenings   Map 5-108
Pub Hours
Credit Cards: No
10 James St.   **Tel: 836 4678**

NEAL STREET
International £££   Map 5-109
12.30-15.00, 19.15-23.00
Closed Sat, Sun (must book)
Credit Cards: A, AX, B, DC.
26 Neal St.   **Tel: 836 8368**

THEATRES:		
1-7	Adelphi	
3-6	Aldwych	
12-5	Drury Lane	
14-7	Duchess	
16-6	Fortune	
20-5	New London	
26-6	Royalty	
27-5	Royal Opera	
29-7	Savoy	
31-8	Strand	
32-7	Vaudeville	

PICCOLO MONO
Italian ££   Map 5-107
12.00-14.30, 18.00-23.50
Credit Cards: A, AX, B, DC.
31 Catherine St.   **Tel: 836 3609**

PLUMMERS
American-English ££   **Map 7-111**
12.00-14.30, 18.00-23.30
Closed Sat L. Sun (must book)
Credit Cards: A, AX, B, DC.
33 King St.   **Tel: 240 2534**

POONS OF COVENT GARDEN
Chinese £££   **Map 7-112**
Closed Sun.
Advisable to book.
Credit Cards: AX, B, DC.
41 King St.   **Tel: 240 1743**

PORTERS
English £   **Map 7-113**
12.00-23.30
Closed No
Credit Cards: A, B.
17 Henrietta St.   **Tel: 836 6466**

RULES
English £££   **Map 7-115**
12.15-14.30, 18.00-23.15
Closed Sat L. Sun (must book)
Credit Cards: A, AX, DC, Visa.
35 Maiden Lane   **Tel: 836 5314**

SAVOY HOTEL GRILL
International £££*   **Map 7-116**
12.30-14.30, 18.00-23.15
Closed Sat L. Sun
Credit Cards: A, AX, B, DC.
Strand & Embankment   **Tel: 836 4343**

River Restaurant £££*
12.30-17.30, 19.20-23.30
(Dancing from 20.30
Sun 19.00 - 22.00)

HOTELS:

39-5	Drury Lane	44-7	Savoy
40-8	Howard	46-7	Strand
41-7	Pastoria	47-6	Waldorf
42-7	Meridien		

Where to Eat – Strand · Covent Garden

SIMEONI'S
Italian £££　　　　　　**Map 5-117**
12.00-14.30, 18.00-23.15
Closed Sat L. Sun
Credit Cards: A, AX, B, DC.
43 Drury Lane　　　　　**Tel: 836 8296**

SIMPSON'S-IN-THE-STRAND
English £££　　　　　　**Map 7-118**
12.00-15.00, 18.00-22.45
Closed Sun (must book)
Credit Cards: A, B.
100 Strand　　　　　　　**Tel: 836 9112**

SHUTTLEWORTH'S at Aldwych
English ££　　　　　　　**Map 7-95**
17.30-23.00.
Sat 17.30-23.30
Credit Cards: A, AX, B, DC.
1 Aldwych　　　　　　　**Tel: 836 3346**

STRAND PALACE HOTEL
Coffee Shop £　　　　　**Map 7-119**
7.00-00.30
Italian Connection ££
Closed Sun
Credit Cards: A, AX, B, DC.
Mash Bar Pub hours
L'Osteria Bar
Carvery Rest. 12.00-14.30, 18.00-22.00
Coffee Shop 11.30-23.30　**Tel: 836 8080**

SHERLOCK HOLMES (Pub &
Restaurant)
Buffet £　　　　　　　　**Map 19-4**
Pub hours
Closed No
Credit Cards: No
10 Northumberland St.　**Tel: 930 2644**

THE GRILL
English £　　　　　　　**Map 7-92**
12.00-24.00. 7 days a week
Credit Cards: A, AX, B, DC.
30 Wellington St.　　　**Tel: 240 7529**

THEATRES:
1-7	Adelphi	20-5	New London
3-6	Aldwych	26-6	Royalty
12-5	Drury Lane	27-5	Royal Opera
14-7	Duchess	29-7	Savoy
16-6	Fortune	31-8	Strand
		32-7	Vaudeville

THE OPERA TERRACE
RESTAURANT AND CAFE
Restaurant English ££   **Map 7-114**
Cafe £
11.30-15.00,
17.30-23.30
Credit Cards: A, AX, B, DC.
45 East Terrace,
Piazza   **Tel: 379 0666**

THE OPERA TAVERN
English £   **Map 5-120**
12.00-23.00
Credit Cards: A, AX, B, DC.
23 Catherine St.   **Tel: 836 7321**

QUINCEY'S
French £££   **Map 7-121**
12.00-14.30,
18.00-23.15
Closed Sun and Sat Lunch
(book rec.)
Credit Cards: A, AX, B, DC.
36 Tavistock St.   **Tel: 240 3972**

VOLTAIRES (Wine Bar)
Buffet £   **Map 7-125**
11.00-15.00,
17.30-23.00
Closed Sun
Credit Cards: Most
41 Maiden Lane   **Tel: 240 7747**

WALDORF HOTEL
Palm Court ££   **Map 6-123**
English
Early till late
Sun 10.30-12.00
Tea
15.30-18.00
Credit Cards: A, AX, B, DC.
Footlights Bar
Pub hours
Closed Sat & Sun
Aldwych   **Tel: 836 2400**

HOTELS:

39-5	Drury Lane	44-7	Savoy
40-8	Howard	46-7	Strand
41-7	Pastoria	47-6	Waldorf
42-7	Meridien		

159

Where to Eat – South Bank

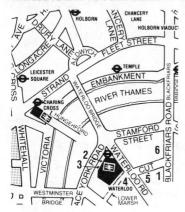

Royal Festival Hall

CAFETERIA
Buffet £
10.00-18.00 Fri, Sat and
Sun 10.00-20.00
Credit Cards: No

FOYERS
Buffet £
10.00-20.00, Sun 12.00-20.00
Credit Cards: A, AX, B, DC.
Tel: 928 3246

National Theatre

OVATIONS RESTAURANT
Dinner - 17.30-23.00. Closed Sun. Sat
Buffet L. 15.15-14.30   **Tel: 928 2033**

LYTTLETON THEATRE
Long Bar - Pub hours. Closed Sun.
Box Office Buffet - 10.00-23.00 Closed
Sun. *Circle Bar* - Perf. days only,
17.30 to end of interval. *Buffet* - 12.00-
20.00. Closed Sun.

OLIVIER THEATRE
Bars and buffets open performance days only.
Two Stalls Bars - 18.00 to end of last
interval. *Two Mezzanine Buffets* -
From 1½ hours before performance.
Circle Bar - 18.00 to end of interval.

COTTESLOE THEATRE
Open from 1½ hours before
performance until int. *Bars & Buffet.*

ACROPOLIS
Greek ££ (for parties)   1
9.00-21.00 (later if book)
Closed Sun
Credit Cards: No
43 The Cut   **Tel: 928 3689**

CAFE DE LA GARE
French ££   2
12.00-22.00
Closed Sat, Sun (must book)
Credit Cards: All
19 York Road   **Tel: 928 9761**

IL PAPAGALLO
Italian ££   3
12.00-24.00. Closed Sun
Credit Cards: Most
35 York Road   **Tel: 928 1003**

LA BARCA
Italian ££   4
12.00-14.30, 19.00-23.30
Closed Sat L. Sun (must book)
Credit Cards: A, AX, B, DC.
81 Lower Marsh   **Tel: 261 9221**

MESON DON FILIP (Wine Bar)
Buffet £   5
Pub hours. Closed Sat. Sun
Credit Cards: No
53 The Cut

SOUTH OF THE BORDER
International ££   6
12.00-14.30, 18.00-23.30
Closed Sat L. Sun
Credit Cards: A, AX, B, DC.
8 Joan St.   **Tel: 928 6374**

THE ARCHDUKE (Wine Bar)
Buffet ££ Restaurant   7
11.00-15.00, 17.30-23.00
Closed Sat L. Sun
Credit Cards: A, AX, B, DC.
Belvedere Road   **Tel: 928 9370**

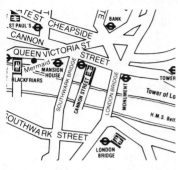

Mermaid Theatre

BUFFET BAR
Buffet £
12.00-14.30, 17.00-21.30
Closed Sun
Credit Cards: No

BRIDGE & DOCKYARD BARS
Pub hours

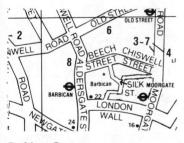

Barbican Centre

THE CUT ABOVE
English ££
12.00-15.00, 17-00-½ hour after the
end of last performance.
Reservations advisable.
Credit Cards: A, AX, B, DC.
Level 7   **Tel: 588 3008**

THE WATERSIDE CAFE
Buffet £
10.00-20.00,
Sun 12.00-20.00
Credit Cards: A, AX, B, DC.
Level 5   **Tel: 638 4141 Ext 350**

WINE ON SIX (Wine Bar)
5.30-9.00pm Mon-Sat
Credit Cards: No
Level 6
There are bars, coffee and snack bars in
the Foyers – Barbican Hall and
Barbican Theatre, Levels 3, 5, 6. Some
keep pub hours, others open for
performances only.

CORNEY & BARROW
(also Wine Bar)
British-French ££   **4**
11.30-15.00, 17.00-20.30
Closed Sat & Sun
(must book)
Credit Cards: A, AX, B, DC.
118 Moorgate   **Tel: 628 2898**

RAVELLO
Italian ££   **6**
12.00-15.00, 18.00-23.30
Closed Sun (must book)
Credit Cards: A, AX, B, DC.
42 Old St.   **Tel: 253 6279**

THE KING'S HEAD (Pub)
Sandwiches   **7**
Pub hours to 19.30
Closed No
Credit Cards: No
Chiswell St.   **Tel: 606 9158**

TRATTORIA VENEZIA
Italian ££   **8**
12.00-15.00, 18.00-23.30
Closed Sat L. Sun
(booking advisable)
Credit Cards: A, AX, B, DC.
5 Goswell Road   **Tel: 253 5063**

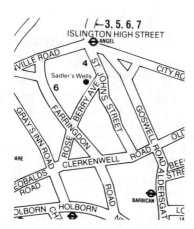

SHAKESPEARE'S HEAD
Pub   6
Pub Hours – Pub Food
1 Arlington Way   **Tel: 837 2581**

UPPERS
Bistro £   7
12.00-24.00
Credit Cards: A, AX, B, DC.
348/349 Upper St.   **Tel: 226 5650**

FREDERICK'S
French £££   3
12.00-14.30, 19.00-23.30
Closed Sun (must book)
Credit Cards: A, AX, B, DC.
Camden Passage   **Tel: 359 2888**

LAKORN THAI
Thai £   4
12.00-15.00, 18.00-23.50
Credit Cards: A, AX, B, DC.
197/199 Rosebery Ave   **Tel: 837 5048**

PORTOFINO
Italian-French ££   5
12.30-15.00, 18.30-23.30
Closed Sun (must book)
Credit Cards: A, AX, B, DC.
39 Camden Passage   **Tel: 226 0884**

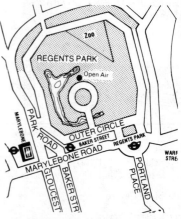

OPEN AIR THEATRE
Cold Buffet & Barbecue £
18.45-22.30
Closed Sun
Credit Cards: No
Bar
18.45-24.00

162

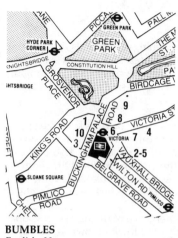

BUMBLES
English ££ 1
12.15-14.15, 18.00-22.30
Closed Sat L. Sun (must book)
Credit Cards: A, AX, B, DC.
16 Buckingham Pal. Rd. **Tel: 828 2903**

GRAN PARADISO
Italian £££ 2
12.00-14.30, 18.15-23.15
Closed Sat L. Sun
Credit Cards: A, AX, B, DC.
52 Wilton Road **Tel: 828 5818**

MASSIMO
Seafood-Game £££ 3
12.00-14.30, 18.15-23.00
Closed Sun (must book)
Credit Cards: A, AX, B, DC.
42 Buckingham Pal. Rd. **Tel: 834 8283**

McDONALD'S
American £ 4
10.00-23.00
Closed No
Credit Cards: No
155 Victoria St.

MIMMO & PASQUALE
Italian £££ 5
12.00-14.30,
18.30-23.00
Closed Sun (must book)
Credit Cards: All
64 Wilton Rd **Tel: 828 6908**

OVERTONS
Seafood £££ 6
12.00-14.30,
17.30-22.30
Closed Sun (must book)
Credit Cards: A, AX, B, DC.
4 Victoria Bldgs. **Tel: 834 3774**

PIZZA EXPRESS
Pizza £ 7
12.00-24.00
Closed No
Credit Cards: A, AX, B.
74 Victoria St.

BIGUNS RIBS
English ££ 8
11.30-23.30
Closed No
Credit Cards: A.
124 Victoria St. **Tel: 834 7350**

TAVOLA CALDA
Italian £ 9
12.00-23.00
Closed Sun
Credit Cards: No
3 Bressenden Place **Tel: 834 5650**

TILES (Wine Bar)
Buffet £ 10
12.00-15.00,
17.30-23.00
Closed Sat, Sun
Credit Cards: A, AX, B, DC.
36 Buckingham Palace Rd.
 Tel: 834 7761

The Theatrical Capital of the World

Today, over four centuries after the opening of London's first theatre, the West End alone has some 50 theatres and concert halls (not counting fringe theatres, of which there are more than 20) ranging from the minute to the majestic, from the classical to the modern.

In the beginning

Although the Romans had introduced their own style of theatre to Britain (the remains of a Roman theatre can still be seen at St. Albans in Hertfordshire), the actual origins of our theatrical tradition can probably be attributed largely to the church. In the 10th century, priests used dramatised performances to teach bible stories and from these developed full-length 'Miracle Plays' which were presented annually to coincide with town festivals.

The early 16th century saw the emergence of the first professional actors who travelled in small groups from town to town — acting in the town squares, in the great houses of the rich and in the yards of the local inns. In 1576 London's first permanent theatre building "The Theatre" was opened in Holywell Lane, Shoreditch — pre-dating Elizabethan drama as we know it today and offering such entertainment as tumbling, vaulting, fencing and rope-dancing. Due to constant criticism from the local authorities, however, it was forced to close — and was eventually dismantled and moved, piece by piece, to Bankside, an area on the south bank of the Thames close to London Bridge.

The Globe Theatre

The materials rescued from "The Theatre" were used to build the famous Globe Theatre, the opening of which in 1599 heralded a flourishing period for live entertainment of all kinds in this part of London. Although little remains today, the fascinating Bear Gardens Museum records in great detail the character and style of the Bankside theatres.

These theatres, of course, also provided a natural outlet for such great writers of the day as Shakespeare, Marlowe and Ben Johnson. Theatre-building too, took on a new importance and was greatly influenced by continental designs. The practice of Italian courtiers of presenting their own grand form of entertainment was introduced to England by the architect Inigo Jones, whose designs for plays proved extremely popular in the courts of James I and Charles I — and whose influence was to last for the next 300 years. In 1642, however, the Puritan regime introduced the Suppression of Theatres Act. Unfortunately, no theatres survived this period which lasted only until 1660 when Charles II came to the throne and encouraged a revival.

The Restoration
The first Restoration theatres were built in the Covent Garden area, which rapidly became the centre of London's theatre-land — and has remained so ever since. The most notable were built on the sites now occupied by The Theatre Royal, Drury Lane and The Royal Opera House, Covent Garden. Each has become a national institution in its own right — the former being recognised as the primary house for stage musicals and the latter for its fine operatic productions and, of course, as the home of the Royal Ballet Company.

As a result of the influx of actors, artistes and their less attractive following in the 18th and 19th centuries, the elite moved away from Covent Garden towards Mayfair — soon to be followed by an ever increasing number of West End theatres, many of which have now disappeared.

As theatres became more and more accessible to the general public and less the private preserve of the well-to-do, so the buildings increased in size, to accommodate larger audiences and to provide additional revenue for financing the more extravagant productions which were now demanded.

The Music Hall
The 19th century was also the heyday of the actor-manager — bringing fame and fortune to such as Sir Henry Irving, William Macready and Frank Benson, whose main following was among the middle classes. It was primarily to cater for the tastes of the working classes that public houses were obliged to put on entertainment — and this, in turn, led to the birth of the Music Hall. Happily, The Players Theatre, recently re-opened, carries on the music hall tradition. There is the Wilton's Music Hall, near Tower Bridge, which, it is hoped will one day re-open.

The West End Theatre today
Most of the theatres which have survived to the present day were built at the turn of the century.

Notable features of London's recent theatrical history have been The New London, the rebuilding of The Mermaid, The National Theatre on the south bank and, in 1982, the exciting new arts complex at the Barbican — which is the home of the Royal Shakespeare Company in London and the London Symphony Orchestra.

Where to Stay

Hotels Central London

The following list includes only those hotels which are located in or around London's West End theatreland – but nevertheless offers a wide choice of recommended traditional and contemporary accommodation at all price levels. For details of hotels outside the area which offer a range of accommodation and prices comparable to those found in any major city, contact The London Tourist Board at Victoria Railway Station – where you will also be able to make your reservation. The opening hours are 9.00-22.30 hrs.

Hotel ratings: ★★★★★ Luxury ★★★★ First Class
★★★ Very Comfortable ★★ Good Average
Note: Add prefix 071 when dialling outside the London Area.

ATHENAEUM ★★★★ Map 3
116 Piccadilly, W1V 0BJ
Tel: 499 3464 Fax: 493 1860 Cable: Acropolis London W1
Rank Hotel. 112 rooms. One of London's newer hotels, which in its design gives full consideration to a gracious and comfortable English style. The theme is continued into the restaurant with its traditional English dishes and international cuisine. The bar is reminiscent of a 19th century Club. 3 suites are designed to cater for private meetings, luncheons and dinner parties.

BERKSHIRE HOTEL ★★★★ Map 4
Oxford Street, W1N 0BY
Tel: 629 7474 Telex: 22270 Fax: 629 8156
Elegant with 147 rooms, each with private bathroom and shower. Cocktail bar and Restaurant.

BERKELEY ★★★★★ Map 3
Wilton Place, SW1X 7RL
Tel: 235 6000 Telex: 919252 Fax: 235 4300 Cable: Silentium London SW1
Savoy Group of Hotels. 160 rooms. Behind the modern exterior of this luxury hotel, elegance and comfort abound. Bedrooms are tastefully furnished. Amenities include swimming pool and poolside bar, saunas, massage rooms, private cinema, main Restaurant and The Buttery. Service, impeccable and unobtrusive.

BRITANNIA INTER-CONTINENTAL ★★★★ Map 1
Grosvenor Square, W1A 3AN
Tel: 629 9400 Telex: 23941 Fax: 629 7736
Inter-Continental. 356 rooms. Georgian style building with all modern comforts. Amenities: Anglo-American restaurant and bar, Waterloo Despatch Pub, Shogun-Japanese restaurant, piano bar, business centre, shopping arcade, conference and banqueting facilities for 120 people.

Hotels

BROWN'S ★★★★   Map 3
Albemarle Street/Dover Street, W1A 4SW
Tel: 493 6020 Telex: 28686 Fax: 493 9381 Cable: Brownotel London W1
Trust Houses Forte. 132 rooms. One of London's traditional hotels that has maintained high standards of service and comfort. Each bedroom has its own charm and style. Of interest there is the St. George's Bar and L'Aperitif Restaurant. Private reception rooms are available for private luncheons and dinners, wedding receptions up to 150 persons.

CAVENDISH ★★★★   Map 3
Jermyn Street, SW1Y 6JF
Tel: 930 2111 Telex: 263187 Fax: 839 2125 Cable: Rosatel
Trust Houses Forte. 255 rooms. In the past, the original hotel was very popular with Royalty – today ideals are kept alive in service, cuisine and atmosphere. Rebuilt in 1966, it is run with efficiency, elegance and style offering round-the-clock service. There is the Sub Rosa bar and not to be forgotten, the Miller's Restaurant, open 7 days a week. Private rooms cater for meetings, lunches, celebration parties and intimate dinners in an elegant style.

CHARING CROSS ★★★   Map 4
Strand, WC2N 5HX
Tel: 839 7282 Telex: 261101 Fax: 839 3933
British Transport Hotels. 210 rooms. Comfortable and convenient. All bedrooms have private bath or shower. Elegant Edwardian decor in the Rendezvous Bar. Comfortable, elegant surrounds in the Betjeman Carving Restaurant, Pilgrims and Pullman Bars. Banqueting and conference facilities for 150.

CHESTERFIELD ★★★★   Map 3
34-36 Charles Street, W1X 8LX
Tel: 491 2622 Telex: 269394 Fax: 491 4793 Cable: Chesotel London W1
87 rooms. A 1747 gracious town house which has been redesigned into a comfortable hotel without losing the charm of the Regency period. The Terrace Bar has historical interest. Butlers Restaurant offers buffet luncheons and traditional French and English dishes for dinners.

CHURCHILL ★★★★★   Map 1
Portman Square, W1A 4ZX
Tel: 486 5800 Telex: 264831 Fax: 935 0431 Cable: Churchotel London W1
489 rooms. Contemporary luxury hotel. Though large, the service is geared to individual requirements including 24-hour full menu room service. For informal meals The Greenery – and for formal occasions The Regency style Arboury. The Churchill Bar has Oriental sporting scenes around the walls and a pianist six nights a week. Elegant and varied conference and banqueting facilities for 30-350.

Hotels

CLARIDGES ★★★★   Map 1
Brook Street, W1A 2JQ
Tel: 629 8860 Telex: 21872 Fax: 499 2210 Cable: Claridges
Savoy Hotels. 205 rooms. The ultimate in luxury, this hotel epitomises English tradition, with all its elegance and comfort. Frequented by Royalty, Rulers and the famous.

CLIFTON-FORD ★★★★   Map 1
Welbeck Street, London W1M 8DN
Tel: 486 6600 Telex: 22569 Fax: 486 7492 Cable: Clifinton London W1
Comfortable modern hotel. Bar, good Restaurant for English food, 24 hour room service, conference facilities.

CONNAUGHT ★★★★★   Map 1
Carlos Place, W1Y 6AL
Tel: 499 7070 Cable: Chataigne, London
90 rooms. Enjoys an International reputation for its unostentatious luxury, peaceful old Manor House charm and efficient service. The bar, restaurant and grill are renowned. Reservations way in advance advisable.

CUMBERLAND ★★★   Map 1
Marble Arch, W1A 4RF
Tel: 262 1234 Telex: 22215 Fax: 724 4621 Cable: Cumberotel, London W1
Trust Houses Forte. 910 rooms. Large modern hotel with extensive facilities. These include The Carvery for meat specialities, "The Coffee Shop" for informality, The Wyvern Restaurant for something special – and the Nocturne Bar – one of three cocktail bars. Various conference and banqueting facilities accommodating 20-330.

DORCHESTER ★★★★★   Map 3
Park Lane, W1A 2HJ
Tel: 629 8888 Telex: 887704 Fax: 409 0114 Cable: Dorch-Hotel London
283 rooms. One of the world's great luxury hotels will re-open 1990 continuing the best traditions of British hospitality, comfort and service. A new oriental restaurant is planned among other innovations but this luxurious hotel will still keep its special particular charm.

DRURY LANE ★★★   Map 2
10 Drury Lane, High Holborn, WC2B 5RE
Tel: 836 6666 Telex: 8811395 Fax: 831 1548 Cable: Drutel London WC2
Grand Metropolitan. 128 rooms. One of London's newest, modern and comfortable hotels with relaxing atmosphere extended throughout. Maudie's Restaurant and Bar and 24-hour room and lounge service. Conference and banqueting facilities for 50-150.

Hotels

DUKES ★★★★   Map 3
St. James' Place, SW1A 1NY Tel: 491 4840 Tlx: 28283 Fax: 493 1264 Cable: Dukeshotel
56 rooms. Built in 1908, in an area of London steeped in history, pageantry and
culture. Elegance is its keynote and the best of modern facilities are blended with
traditional service, courtesy and decor. The Duke's Bar and St. James' Room
Restaurant are widely renowned for their friendly atmosphere and fine food. An
elegant banqueting suite is available for private functions.

LONDON MARRIOTT HOTEL ★★★★   Map 1
Grosvenor Square, W1A 4AW Tel: 493 1232 Telex: 268101 Lonmar G Fax: 491 3201
Marriott Hotels and Resorts. 229 rooms. Completely refurbished during 1984 bringing
this ideally situated hotel up to four star standards. Diplomat-Grill and Bar on Grosvenor Square and the Regent Lounge. Conference and banquet facilities for 30-500.

GROSVENOR HOUSE ★★★★★   Map 1
Park Lane, W1A 3AA Tel: 499 6363 Tlx: 24871 Fax: 493 3341 Cbl: Grovhows Ldn W1
Trust Houses Forte. 478 rooms. Another traditionally famous hotel which has been
refurbished at a cost of millions of pounds, resulting in a style of informal
elegance throughout. Its amenities include The Park Lounge, Red Room (Bar),
Italian/French/English restaurants and Expresso Coffee Shop, not forgetting the
exceptional indoor swimming pool, gymnasium and health club. Banqueting
and conference facilities cater for up to 2,200.

HILTON ★★★★★   Map 3
Park Lane, W1A 2HH Tel: 493 8000 Tlx: 24873 Fax: 493 4957 Cable: Hiltels London
510 rooms. A comtemporary hotel geared to today's needs whilst to a great extent
retaining style and atmosphere. Used extensively for International business, a
convention and meeting centre. Rooms generally large and well appointed.
There are five bars and four restaurants. Well known are the Roof Restaurant for
dining and supper dancing. Trader Vic's Polynesian Restaurant and the Scand-
inavian Sandwich Shop. Banquet and convention facilities for 50-1,000.

HOLIDAY INN MAYFAIR ★★★★   Map 3
Berkeley St./Piccadilly/London W1X 6NE
Tel: 493 8282 Tlx: 24561 Fax: 629 2827 Holidex: Lonmf
Holiday Inn Hotels Inc. 190 rooms with 7 luxurious suites. Recently refurbished
throughout. Nightingale Restaurant, A la Carte menu, 2 Table D'Hote menus,
and executive luncheon and a traditional Sunday Brunch.

HOSPITALITY INN ★★★   Map 2
39 Coventry St, Piccadilly Circus, W1V 8EL Tel: 930 4033 Tlx: 24616 Fax: 925 2586
Mt. Charlotte Group. 92 rooms. Comfortable rooms. Modern design. Cocktail Bar
and Coffee Shop.

HOWARD ★★★★★   Map 2
Temple Place, Strand, WC2R 2PR Tel: 836 3555 Telex: 268047 Fax: 379 4547
Barclays Hotel. 141 rooms. This luxury hotel, with panoramic views of the Thames
has a blend of elegant decoration in its public rooms, whilst bedrooms are of
modern luxury and traditional design. Cocktail bar and restaurant serving French
haute cuisine. 24-hour room service.

Hotels

INN ON THE PARK ★★★★★   Map 3
Park Lane, W1A 1AZ
Tel: 499 0888 Telex: 22771 Fax: 493 1895 Cable: Innpark
Four Seasons Hotel. 228 rooms. This luxury hotel in a beautiful setting is one of London's nicest hotels. The richness and comfort extend into its Guest Lounge, Garden Room with garden patio, the famous Four Seasons Restaurant, and the informal Lanes Restaurant. Banqueting, meetings and reception facilities in five rooms can accommodate 40-600.

INTER-CONTINENTAL ★★★★★   Map 3
1 Hamilton Place, Hyde Park Corner, W1V 0QY
Tel: 409 3131 Telex: 25853 Fax: 493 3476 Cable: Hydparcor
500 rooms. This luxury air conditioned hotel has the best to offer. Rooms designed for modern comfort. Seventh Floor Hamiltons Supper Club with wonderful views over London, live entertainment and night-time disco dancing. The Coffee House Restaurant with its 18th century atmosphere, the Le Soufflé Restaurant, famous for its French cuisine. Meeting rooms for everything from a small strategy session to a conference for 750 with simultaneous translation in the ballroom. Garage under hotel.

LONDONER ★★★   Map 1
Welbeck Street, W1M 8HS
Tel: 935 4442 Telex: 894630 Fax: 487 3782 Cable: Superotel London W1
142 rooms all with private facilities. Colour television and direct dial telephones. Amenities include a bar and Oliver's Restaurant. Also 24 hour lounge and Room Service.

LONDONDERRY ★★★★★   Map 3
Park Lane, W1Y 8AP
Tel: 493 7292 Telex: 263292 Fax: 495 1395
140 rooms. A luxurious hotel in Italian Renaissance style. Delightful Piano Bar. All-day restaurant and evening Grill.

MANDEVILLE ★★★   Map 1
Mandeville Place, London W1M 6BE
Tel: 935 5599 Telex: 2649487 Fax: 935 9588 Cables: Manvilhote London W1
Executive Hotels. 163 bedrooms all with bath and shower, well furnished, colour television with free in-house movies, dial direct telephone etc., Boswell's Pub, La Cocotte Cocktail Bar, Orangery Coffee House, La Cocotte Mediterranean a la carte restaurant, 24-hour lounge and room service.

MAYFAIR ★★★★★   Map 3
Berkeley Street, W1A 2AN
Tel: 629 7777 Telex: 262526 Fax: 629 1459 Cable: Mayfairtel London W1
Grand Metropolitan. 330 rooms. One of London's older hotels, well known for its amenities and comfort. The Chateaubriand Restaurant for good food and elegant dining, 9 banqueting suites, the Mayfair Theatre which seats 310 for special events and the Starlight Cinema.

Hotels

LE MERIDIEN ★★★★★ Map 2
Piccadilly, W1V 0BH Tel: 734 8000 Telex: 25795 Fax: 437 3574
284 rooms. Has been totally refurbished and now a really de-luxe hotel. Much of
the granduer of the past still being retained. Spacious bedrooms each with bath,
beautifully furnished. The Oak Room (gourmet) restaurant, French style cuisine
and the less expensive Terrace Garden Restaurant and the Brazzerie open from
7.00-23.50. Dining facilities for 450 and conference facilities available.

MOSTYN ★★★ Map 1
Portman Street, W1H 0DE
Tel: 935 2361 Telex: 27656 Fax: 487 2759 Cable: Mostyno London W1
Grand Metropolitan. 107 rooms, tastefully furnished, most with separate bath-
room and shower. Brummels Bar and Restaurant. Banqueting and conference
facilities for 10-100.

MOUNT ROYAL ★★★ Map 1
Marble Arch, W1A 4UR Tel: 629 8040 Tlx: 23355 Fax: 499 7792 Cbl: Mounroy Ldn W1
Mount Charlotte Hotels. 700 rooms. Well decorated spacious rooms, all with
private bathroom and shower and colour TV. Harry's Bar, Coffee House and
Terrace Grill Restaurant. Conference and banqueting facilities for 1,500.

PARK LANE ★★★★ Map 3
Tel: 499 6321 Telex: 21533 Fax: 499 1965 Cable: Parlanotel Piccadilly, W1Y 8BX
54 suites and 270 rooms. One of London's older and more stylish hotels. All
bedrooms have a bathroom en suite, double glazing, direct dial telephone, mini
bar, colour television, radio and 24 hour room service. Bracewells and the Garden
Room Restaurants, The Bar and The Palm Court Lounge, Brazzerie on the Park –
lovely for pre-theatre meal. Banqueting and conference facilities.

PASTORIA ★★★ Map 2
St. Martin's Street, WC2H 7HL
Tel: 930 8641 Telex: 25538 Fax: 925 0551 Cable: Heartowest London WC2
Sarova Group. 52 rooms. A small friendly hotel with a family atmosphere and
comfortable bedrooms. Bar and lounge are pleasant for relaxing, with tasty
snacks served in the restaurant.

PORTMAN (Situated in the heart of theatreland) ★★★★ Map 1
22 Portman Square, W1H 9FL
Tel: 486 5844 Telex: 261526 Fax: 935 0537 Cable: Inhotelcor
Inter-Continental. 278 rooms. Fully air-conditioned rooms with mini-bars, colour
television, free in-house movies, and built in hairdryers in all bath-rooms. 24-
hour room service. Portman Corner – Pub and Bakery, Truffles French
Restaurant. Bar Normande, Rotisserie Normand. Conference facilities for up to
600 persons.

RAMADA ★★★★ Map 1
Berners Street, W1A 3BE
Tel: 636 1629 Telex: 25759 Fax: 580 3972 Cable: Ramhl London
237 rooms. Built in 1909 it still retains its Edwardian elegance and charm. Lounge
bar, restaurant, conference and reception facilities for 10-150.

Hotels

REGENT PALACE ★★   Map 1
Piccadilly Circus, W1R 6EP
Tel: 734 7000 Telex: 23740 Fax: 734 6435 Cable: Regentotel
Trust Houses Forte. 1,002 rooms. Busy, very popular and well run with friendly atmosphere. Many bars and restaurants including the Carvery.

THE RITZ (Deluxe) **★★★★★**   Map 3
Piccadilly, W1V 9DG
Tel: 493 8181 Telex: 267200 Fax: 493 2687 Cable: Riztotel
Remains a magnificent and luxurious hotel. Renowned high standard of service is maintained in majestic setting. Experience the sheer beauty of the Palm Court for afternoon tea. The Restaurant, with its beautiful decor and lavish ceiling paintings has always been the rendezvous of important figures from all walks of life.

ROYAL ADELPHI ★★   Map 4
21-23 Villiers Street, WC2N 6ND
Tel: 930 8764 Fax: 930 8735
55 rooms. Situated next to Charing Cross Station – inexpensive catering for the tourist and businessman.

ROYAL HORSEGUARDS THISTLE HOTEL ★★★★   Map 4
2A Whitehall Court, SW1A 2EJ
Tel: 839 3400 Telex: 917096 Fax: 925 2263
Thistle Hotel. 280 rooms. Smart, well furnished with modern comforts. Spacious lounge, Granby's Restaurant and river front terrace. Conference and reception facilities.

ROYAL TRAFALGAR THISTLE HOTEL ★★★   Map 4
Whitcomb St, Trafalgar Square, WC2H 7HG
Tel: 930-4477 Telex: 24616 Fax: 925 2149
108 rooms, modern hotel used by businessmen and tourists. Has its own English Pub, Lounge and new Brasserie and Cocktail Bar.

SAVOY ★★★★★   Map 2
Strand, WC2R 0EU
Tel: 836 4343 Telex: 24234 Fax: 240 6040
200 rooms. Luxurious and renowned for its excellence throughout. 24-hour room service is only one of its many special services. Conference and entertaining facilities range from most intimate and elegant private dining rooms to the Lancaster Room which accommodates 500 people. The Savoy Theatre is part of this complex.

Hotels

ST. GEORGE'S ★★★★   Map 1
Langham Place, Oxford Circus, W1N 8QS
Tel: 580 0111 Telex: 27274 Fax: 436 7997 Cable: St. George's Hotel London W1
Trust Houses Forte (UK) Ltd. 85 rooms. Modern most comfortable tower-like construction with excellent view of the City from public rooms. The Summit Restaurant on the 15th floor is renowned for its good food.

STAFFORD ★★★★   Map 3
16 St. James's Place, SW1A 1NJ
Tel: 493 0111 Telex: 28602 Fax: 493 7121 Cable: Staforotel
61 rooms. Peacefully situated, this converted mansion offers the best in English tradition. Gracefully furnished throughout. American Bar and Restaurant of high repute. Banqueting facilities for 10-50.

STRAND PALACE ★★★   Map 2
Strand, WC2R 0JJ
Tel: 836 8080 Telex: 24208 Fax: 836 2077 Cable: Luxury London WC2R 0JJ
Trust Houses Forte. 770 rooms. Large practical and convenient hotel with all the necessary amenities, well known cocktail bar, coffee shop, Carvery for fixed price meals, hot and cold buffet, Italian Connection restaurant off Covent Garden with Pizzeria, Piazza and L'Osteria Bar. Conference and entertainment facilities for 20-200.

WALDORF ★★★★   Map 2
Aldwych, WC2B 4DD
Tel: 836 2400 Telex: 24574 Fax: 836 7244 Cable: Waldorfius
Trust Houses Forte. 310 rooms. An Edwardian style hotel which has been carefully redecorated to retain its original elegance. Well appointed public rooms, bars, well known Palm Court Lounge and Waldorf Restaurant. Conference and reception facilities are varied and numerous.

WASHINGTON ★★★   Map 3
5/7 Curzon Street, W1Y 8DT
Tel: 499 7030 Telex: 24540 Fax: 495 6172 Cable: Georgotel London W1
Sarova Hotels. 159 rooms. Public rooms are pleasant and comfortable. Madison's Restaurant and Lounge Bar. Conference and reception facilities for 30-250.

WESTBURY ★★★★   Map 1
New Bond Street at Conduit Street, London W1A 4UH
Tel: 629-7755 Telex: 24378 Fax: 495 1163
A luxury hotel situated in the heart of fashionable Mayfair. 242 bedrooms including 14 suites. All rooms have private bath and shower, remote control colour television, direct dial telephone, 24 hour room service. Public rooms include Polo Bar, Restaurant and 24 hour lounge. Conference and banqueting suites available to accommodate from 10-100 people.

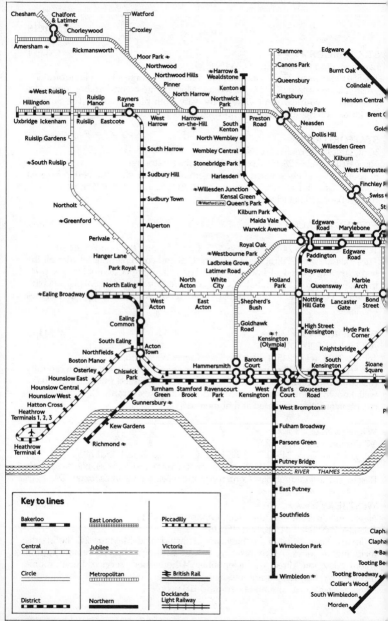

Key to lines

Bakerloo	East London	Piccadilly
Central	Jubilee	Victoria
Circle	Metropolitan	⇌ British Rail
District	Northern	Docklands Light Railway

©Copyright London Regional Transport

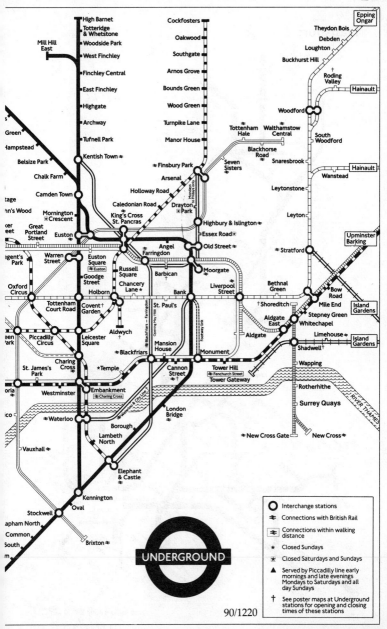

Transport

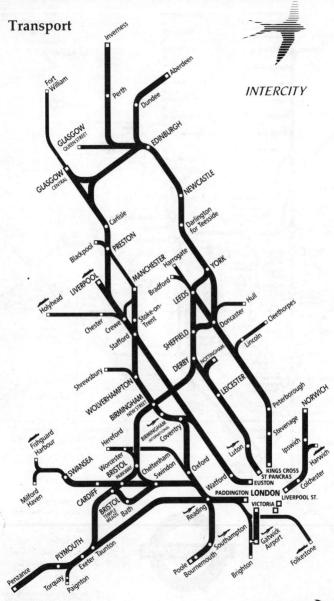

INTERCITY

© British Railways Board 1989/90

TLB/90/2305